W9-BSV-648

Gas. *Station* COLLECTIBLES

A WALLACE-HOMESTEAD PRICE GUIDE

Gas.
Station
COLLECTIBLES

Mark Anderton
Sherry Mullen

099070

Wallace-Homestead Book Company
Radnor, Pennsylvania

ACKNOWLEDGMENTS

We would like to recognize these very important people for their aid in completion of this book: Mr. Harry Rinker who initially encouraged us to do this project, Mr. Bruce Robinson for his friendship and knowledge of the hobby, and Dr. Dan Hardesty of Dynamite Auction Co. for his unselfish help and inspiration. I, Mark, would like to personally acknowledge my Dad for all those reasons you normally list and then some, to my wife for just being herself, and to my sister for helping out in a critical time in my life.

We would also like to thank the consignors who trusted our young company to photograph, describe, and sell their prized collections through our auction house. And, of course, we send our thanks to our cherished customers without whom none of this would have been possible.

Published in Radnor, Pennsylvania 19089, by Wallace-Homestead, a division of Chilton Book Company

Signs on the cover appear courtesy of Ted Swain; the "Blue Crown Spark Plugs" package and "Mobilgas Road Maps" display are from the Raymond E. Holland Automotive Art Collection.

Designed by Anthony Jacobson

Manufactured in the United States of America

Library of Congress Cataloging-in-Publication Data

Anderton, Mark.
    Gas station collectibles / Mark Anderton, Sherry Mullen.
        p.   cm.
    Includes bibliographical references and index.
    ISBN 0-87069-705-6
    1. Service stations—Collectibles—United States—Catalogs.
    2. Petroleum industry and trade—Collectibles—United States—
    Catalogs. I. Mullen, Sherry. II. Title.
    NK808.A54   1993
    629.28′6′0973075—dc20   93-31790
                                                        CIP

1 2 3 4 5 6 7 8 9 0   2 1 0 9 8 7 6 4 5 3

Contents

Introduction   **1**

1 Fill It Up: Gas Pumps, Gas Globes, and Pump Plates   **9**

Gas Pumps   10
Gas Globes   14
Pump Plates   22

2 Pour It On: Oil Cans of All Sizes   **27**

One-Quart Cans   28
Five-Quart Cans   37
Half-Gallon Cans   41
One-Gallon Cans   43
Two-Gallon Cans   48
Five-Gallon Cans   58
Five-Gallon Easy-Pour Cans   62

3 From Hood to Tailpipe: Car Care Products in Individual Containers   **65**

Car Cleaners   66
Greases and Other Lubricants   68
Antifreezes   73
Engine Products   75

4 A Beacon Along the Way: Signs for Every Purpose   **77**

Painted Metal Signs   78
Painted Tin Signs   80
Flanged Signs   83
Banners   86
Paper Signs   87
Cardboard Signs   88
Porcelain Signs   89

5 May I Help You? Sales and Service-Related Items — 93

Clocks — 94
Thermometers — 96
Product Displays and Salesman's Samples — 99
Hats — 107
Arm Patches — 108
Maps and Map Holders — 110
Miscellaneous — 113

6 Take It Home: Premiums, Giveaways, and Other Souvenirs — 115

Pins — 116
Ashtrays and Lighters — 117
License Plate Attachments — 118
Calendars — 119
Salt and Pepper Shakers — 121
Banks — 122
Toys — 124
Miscellaneous — 126

Appendix A: Abbreviations Used in This Book — 130
Appendix B: A History of the Oil Industry — 131
Appendix C: Collectors' Resources — 148

Bibliography — 149
Index — 150

Introduction

Stopping at a gas station today is usually a quick transaction involving push-button choices of octane grade, payment method, and self-serve or full service. Gas stations, or filling stations as they used to be called, once played a more vital role in the day-to-day life of motorists. Automobiles were repaired and serviced as well as fueled there, and travelers were accommodated in a personal way. Interest in gas station collectibles does not arise only from individual memories of travel and service, however. The image of the bygone gas station also brings to mind a sense of adventure, a pioneering spirit that was evident in the development of the oil and automobile industries and that shaped so much of the fabric of American life in the twentieth century.

The Oil Industry

The oil industry traces its roots to western Pennsylvania,* for it is there, in a little town named Titusville, that Col. Edwin L. Drake drilled the first oil well. Drake was the General Agent of Seneca Oil Company, a company newly formed by several New Haven, Connecticut, businessmen who owned the Pennsylvania Rock Oil Company. He was sent to Titusville in the spring of 1858 to drill for oil. After many unavoidable delays and after overcoming numerous obstacles, Drake began drilling in the summer of 1859. On a Saturday afternoon, August 27, as Drake and his men were about to quit work, the drill dropped into a crevice at a depth of 69 feet. They then pulled out their tools and went home without any thought of having struck oil. Late Sunday afternoon, the driller, William A. Smith, visited the well, peered in the pipe, and saw a dark fluid floating on top of the water. Oil had been struck! Drake had demonstrated a way to secure oil in great abundance (before that time, only surface oil was available from shallow pits dug along the Oil Creek Valley). He had tapped the vast subterranean deposits of petroleum underneath the Oil Creek Valley, and, although oil up to that time had been used for its medicinal and illuminating qualities, it was not long before its lubricating and fuel potential were brought to the fore.

Some of the Pennsylvania and Ohio oil companies that have their roots in this important discovery include Tidewater Oil Company (now known as Getty Oil

---

* See Appendix B for a more thorough discussion of the history of the oil industry.

Company), Pure Oil (now a division of Union Oil Company), John D. Rockefeller's Standard Oil of Cleveland, and later Pennzoil and Continental.

The oil boom spread south and west. The first producing oil well in California was drilled by a Pennsylvanian, Robert McPherson, at Pico Canyon in 1876. A gusher discovered near Los Angeles in 1895 by Lyman Stewart (who, along with W. L. Hardison, had formed the Union Oil Company in 1890) spurred oil seekers to make their way to California. Oil companies with California roots include Socal, Union, Signal, Gilmore, General, Hancock, and Sunset.

Two Pennsylvanians, John H. Galey and James M. Guffey, with the help of Pittsburgh financier Andrew Mellon, bought a previously unsuccessful drilling operation near Beaumont, Texas, and used the latest equipment to strike paydirt. Their efforts culminated in the Gulf Refining Company, which later became Gulf Oil Corporation. A mere 20 miles to the south of this discovery, Joseph S. Cullinan organized the Texas Company, which later became Texaco. Texaco later joined with Gulf and Sun to create the world's largest oil exporting facility at Port Arthur, Texas. It also acquired drilling operations in Wichita Falls, Electra, and Petrolia. These three firms were soon able to supply the Eastern refineries with more oil in one year than Pennsylvania had in the previous ten. Other companies formed in Texas include Texas Pacific, Magnolia, Humble, Panhandle, Waggoner, Golden West, and Pioneer.

Although oil was discovered in Oklahoma as early as 1859 (the same year as Drake's discovery), the state's first producing well was the Nellie Johnson No. 1, which was sunk north of Bartlesville April 15, 1897. The state's first gusher was the Sue Bland No. 1, which started flowing in 1901. Oklahoma's oil boom began in earnest in 1905 with the discovery of the 8,000 acre Glenn Pool field near Tulsa. Competition for leases in this new midcontinent field was fierce and, by 1907, Oklahoma was the top oil producing state. With production at Beaumont falling off, Gulf and Texaco both built pipelines from Port Arthur to the Glenn Pool reserves. Standard Oil also extended its Atlantic pipeline to Oklahoma. Oil companies originating from this area include Phillips, Deep Rock, Skelly, Champlin, Wirt-Franklin, Kanotex, Eason, and Diamond.

Enter the Automobile

The oil industry owes much to Karl Benz, a German engineer who developed the first gasoline-powered motor vehicle in 1885. Frank and Charles Duryea introduced America's first gasoline powered motor vehicle in 1893. By 1900, it was generally thought that the gasoline-powered vehicles were superior to those powered by electricity or steam; but it took Henry Ford to make them popular. Ford introduced mass production into the automobile business, and the idea took off. In 1903, he sold 600 Model A Fords for $850 each. By 1908, he had introduced the Model T, which he manufactured by the assembly-line method. By 1911, more than 500,000 automobiles had been sold in the United States. That year marked the first time most oil companies' gasoline sales were greater than their sales of kerosene.

At first there were over 170 manufacturers of automobiles. Besides Ford, other prominent firms included the Cadillac Manufacturing Company (1902) and the Buick Manufacturing Company (1902). William Durant took over leadership at Buick in 1904 and, in 1908, he filed papers to form the General Motors Corporation. The new corporation started with Buick and Oldsmobile. Oakland and Cadillac joined in 1909. Chevrolet was added in 1918. By 1920, more than 30 companies had joined the General Motors team.

As American auto production increased, so did production of gasoline and motor oil. There is no question that the advent of the auto age made the oil industry the giant that it is today.

Technology kept pace. In the 1910s and 1920s, cars had low compression engines and ran low octane fuel. This changed in 1921 when Thomas Midgley discovered an inexpensive fluid, tetra ethyl lead, which contained certain anti-knock compounds. A teaspoon of this fluid, when added to a gallon of gasoline, increased the octane by 10 points and also eliminated knock in the low compression engines of the day.

In 1923, Midgley assigned his use patent to the General Motors Research Corporation, and Standard Oil of New Jersey gained a process patent for an inexpensive production process. On August 18, 1924, these firms simultaneously combined their patent rights and formed the Ethyl Corporation.

Higher compression engines were developed in the late 1920s and 1930s. These made the cars of that era faster and more powerful. At the same time, oil industry scientists developed thermal and catalytic cracking, a process which resulted in the development of the world's first 100-octane motor fuel. This led eventually to the development of high-grade aviation fuel, which is credited with helping the Allies win World War II.

Getting the Gasoline to the Motorists

Producing gasoline was only half the battle. The oil companies of the 20th century also had to become aggressive marketers. Their customer base, the motorists of America and indeed the world, was vast, and the rewards of capturing healthy shares of this customer base were enormous.

To get the gasoline into the tanks of the nation's cars, the companies first had to distribute it (sometimes on a national scale), then they had to devise facilities to dispense the fuel into the tanks of the cars. At first, gasoline from the refineries was transported by pipeline or rail tank car to bulk oil stations located on the rims of cities and towns. There it was pumped into large, cylindrical drums held above ground. From these above-ground tanks gasoline was gravity-fed into five-gallon measuring cans and then poured through funnels into the automobile's fuel tank. The funnel was usually lined with a heavy rag or chamois to filter out sediment or other foreign materials which might damage the car's engine.

At first, motorists carried extra cans of gasoline with them on their cars; but within a few years the dispensing network of the oil companies became more efficient. Within a few years, gasoline from the bulk tank stations was dispensed into horse-drawn tank wagons and transported to livery stables, blacksmith shops, or general stores where it was stored in tanks that were smaller than the ones seen at the bulk storage facilities. At these locations, motorists would fill their tanks with measuring cans and funnels, following the same procedure as previously outlined. At about this same time, automobile storage and repair garages began to appear. These too sold gasoline.

This procedure was soon superseded by Sylvanus F. Bowser, the man who in 1885 developed a kerosene pump based on the plunger method of drawing water from a well. By 1905 he had refined this pump into one that could dispense either kerosene or gasoline and could be kept outside. The Bowser Self Measuring Gasoline Storage Pump consisted of a square metal tank enclosed in a secure wooden cabinet. The cabinet was equipped with a forced suction pump controlled by a hand-operated lever. It also had a hose attachment which allowed gasoline to be dispensed directly into the automobile fuel tank. These pump cabinets (commonly called "filling stations") were placed primarily at general stores or automobile repair garages.

In 1905, the Automobile Gasoline Company of St. Louis, Missouri, opened the nation's first drive-in filling station. The owner, C. H. Laessig, had rigged up an old upright water heater, a measuring gauge, and an ordinary garden hose to dispense gasoline by gravity feed.

The following year, John A. Tokheim of Cedar Rapids, Iowa, invented the Tokheim Dome Oil Pump. In 1910, the first curbside pumps with underground storage were introduced. Curbside refueling, however, led to traffic congestion. To eliminate this problem, garages began to use self-measuring storage systems which allowed the convenience of indoor refueling with the safety of outdoor storage.

All this led to the world's first true gasoline station, which was opened by the Gulf Oil Corporation on Baum Boulevard in Pittsburgh in December, 1913. This station utilized both modern pumps and an underground storage system. Each of the other major gasoline companies followed soon thereafter with their versions of the gasoline station.

These early stations were company-owned and -operated. Employees working at them were paid a wage by the major oil companies involved. At first they sold gasoline only, but beginning about 1920 they began to add service bays in order to get into automobile repair and maintenance as well as the sale of gasoline.

Meanwhile, a host of independent gasoline retailers got into the business. These were, for example, operators of liveries who simply switched from dealing in horses to dealing in gasoline. The independents grew in numbers but were hampered by the fact that they had to purchase their gasoline from the major companies or through jobbers. Then, in 1928, the Murphy Oil Company of Eldorado, Arkansas, came up with a better idea. This firm developed the concept of "track-siders." These were gasoline sales stations located beside railroad spurs which stored their gasoline in above-ground tanks. The track-siders got their gasoline directly from the railroad tank cars. Thus, they were able to eliminate the middlemen and were therefore able to obtain their gas at lower cost. They in turn passed this savings on to their customers. The track-siders were the first gasoline discounters. The idea caught on like wildfire (especially in the South).

A dramatic change in marketing took place as a result of a little-known tax passed in Iowa in 1935. This was the chain store tax. The major oil companies, which each had dozens of stations throughout Iowa, were faced with enormous tax bills because of this new tax. To get out of paying these bills, the major oil companies got out of the business of operating their own gasoline service stations and instead leased their stations to their operators.

During World War II there was no growth; but, when the war ended, the oil industry expanded tremendously. America built all sorts of new roads during these postwar years and, wherever the new roads appeared, gas stations soon followed. This growth continued through the 1950s, but when gas shortages began to appear in the 1960s and especially in the 1970s, it became evident the industry had overbuilt. There simply were too many gas stations and, as a result, many stations never survived the gas shortages of the 1970s.

These same shortages also prompted the independent stations to adopt another successful marketing technique. The independents (no longer limited to trackside operations) devised the convenience store concept—that is, their stations sold grocery items and other necessities as well as gasoline. This concept proved so popular that the major oil companies adopted this strategy as well. Many of the majors' stations simply converted their auto service bays into convenience store areas.

The major oil companies also began to put the squeeze on the independent stations that obtained their gasoline from the majors. The independent stations found they simply could not get gasoline from the major companies anymore and, as a result, the majors began to take over the independent stations one by one.

By the early 1980s, the major oil companies began to get back into salaried operators once again. When this happened, the oil jobbers began to take over the independent stations.

Advertising, of course, played a major role in the marketing of gasoline. At first, the oil companies did not need to advertise at all. Motorists sought them out—they had to if they wanted to stay on the road. By 1915, however, there were so many motorists on the road that the oil companies realized they had to advertise to retain the customers they had. Between 1915 and 1920, the concept of the gasoline brand was developed. Each company tried to forge its own identity with logos, signs, slogans, etc. Some companies went so far as to put coloring in their gasoline, so that their product could be easily identified through the glass globes on the pumps.

Advertising played a major role in gasoline marketing up to the first real shortage in 1972. Then, companies simply stopped advertising because advertising might be construed as promoting consumption. Because of the shortage, the country wanted conservation—not consumption. Advertising did not really resume until 1975.

In the 1980s, the companies concentrated on improving their image. At many stations, they removed the old signs and the old marquees and replaced them with glitzy, clean-looking new ones, all in an attempt to clean up the company's image.

Although the major oil companies dominated the marketplace, hundreds of smaller firms remained in the business. Some thrived, some didn't.

A typical example was the Continental Refining Co. of Oil City, Pennsylvania. Founded in 1885, Continental refined and marketed lubricating oil, gasoline, and other petroleum-based products under the brand names of Coreco, Pennsyelect, DuPennDo, Continental, and Pennintental.

The firm was founded by Thomas Anderton, an Englishman who immigrated to Pittsburgh in 1862 to join his brother in the cooperage business. His services as a barrel-maker were in demand in the oil fields of Pennsylvania. He labored for a number of oil companies and toiled as a grocer for a few years until, in 1885, he and partners Louis Morris and Louis Waltz organized the Continental Refinery Ltd. After a year, Anderton bought out his partners and changed the name to Continental Refining Co. Waltz, incidentally, formed another partnership a year later to form Penn Refining Works—the company that later became Pennzoil.

When Anderton died in 1915, his three sons, Joseph, Aloysius, and Thomas, Jr., took over the firm. At that time, the business was booming. It had numerous service stations in the immediate Pennsylvania area and another 50 in Canada. By the 1920s, Continental also owned 50 railroad tank cars and collection and shipping activities at the Philadelphia port. However, when the Great Depression struck America, the larger refineries put the squeeze on the smaller ones by limiting the amount of crude oil available on the market. By 1942, Continental and other small refineries had been forced out of business.

That year Continental was purchased out of receivership and joined with other refineries to produce aviation fuel at a newly constructed high octane plant in Rouseville. After the war, the firm's old problem—lack of dependable crude oil sources—resurfaced. The company closed in 1951.

The Collection Craze

In recent years, the collecting of memorabilia from the "good old days" of the oil industry, especially the collection of items from the period of gasoline marketing, has become the rage. Nostalgia is one motivating factor. Some people also collect as an investment and others because their families have been (or are) in the oil industry themselves. People began collecting this kind of material in the 1930s and by the 1970s, collectors started to pool their mutual interests by forming clubs and publishing newsletters. Collectors' conventions became common about 10 years ago, and they continue to this day.

Some collectors look for rarity, others for condition; still others are trying to reconstruct entire gasoline stations. For whatever reason, the collection of oil industry memorabilia has become one of the hottest segments in the collectibles business today. New collectors' clubs and new conventions are springing up all over the country. Globes, pitcher cans, maps, and oil company giveaway items seem to be the most in demand. Some one-gallon cans sell today for as high as $3,000. Globes can go for as high as $15,000, and prices continue to increase drastically. Only one thing is for certain—the market for oil industry collectibles has not yet reached its peak.

In this exciting collecting field, it is important to be an informed collector. Before buying or bidding on an item, the collector must try to determine the condition of the item, its perceived rarity, and the market demand for the item. Knowing which collectors are following or buying that particular item and whether or not the market for the item is on the upswing or a downturn is vital.

Most items in this book have been given a collecting grade from 5 to 10. The grade is usually given for the "Display" aspect, or the *front*, of the item. Occasionally, the back side of the item, or the "Reverse," is also graded. The following table indicates the meaning of each grade.

Grading Guide to Gas Station Collectibles

Grade	Condition	Description
10	Mint	Also known as NOS (new old stock). Items must show no trace of wear. Usually only items that were used just for display purposes qualify for such a high grade.
9	Near Mint	Item may show minor traces of wear, very minor abrasions, and some minor loss of luster. Overall display value is excellent.
8	Very Near Mint	Metal items may have some small dents or wrinkles and light scratches to the surface. Painted items may have minor flaking. Overall display value is fine.
7	Very Good	Item has some wear but still displays nicely. Metal items may have surface rust, wrinkles, dents, or scratching. Painted items may have some loss of luster.
6	Fair	Item has obvious wear. Painted items may be chipped or faded. Metal items may have dents, wrinkles, rust, and scratches.
5	Poor	Painted items may have serious paint loss. Metal items may have heavy pitting, scratches, rust, wrinkles, and even holes. Most collectors would not display an item of this grade.

One of Mark's father's favorite sayings is "There's no substitute for good judgment." We feel this applies here just as it does to all collecting ventures.

Happy hunting!

CHAPTER 1

Fill It Up:

Gas Pumps, Gas Globes, and Pump Plates

Gas pumps have been in use at filling stations since the 1900s. They constitute one of the more expensive collecting categories within gas station collectibles, with pumps from the 1930s and 1940s being especially desirable. Gas globes were introduced as a design element in 1910. Pump plates hung on the side of the pump and identified the oil company.

Gas Pumps

"Atlantic" Gasoline Pump. 80" h. Gold imperial shield on front. Atlantic Globe on top is red, blue, and white. Pump is red. "Martin & Schwartz Inc/ Sallisbury, Maryland U.S.A." Display 9. **$550**

"Conoco Gasoline" Ethyl Gasoline Pump. 60" h. 16½" w. Pump is green on front with yellow sides. Display 9. **$650**

"Esso Extra" Gasoline Pump. 90″ h. 24″ w. 16″ deep. Pump is blue and white and reads ' "Wayne" Fort Wayne, Ind. U.S.A.' Display 9. **$550**

"Gulf" Gasoline Pump. 75″ h. 22″ w. 15″ deep. Pump is orange, white, and blue and reads "Gilbarco Calco-meter." Display 9. **$400**

"Mobilgas Special" Gasoline Pump. 62½" h. 16½" w. White on front with red sides. Display 9. **$700**

"Sinclair Aircraft" Gasoline Pump. 57" h. 16½" w. Green on front with red sides. Display 9. **$650**

"Sunoco Dynafuel" Gasoline Pump. 62" h. 20" w. 16" deep. Pump is blue with yellow trim. "Martin & Schwartz Inc." also appears. Scarce. Display 9. **$950**

"Tioga Gasoline" Pump. 60" h. 15½" w. Silver front with a yellow side. Display 9. **$750**

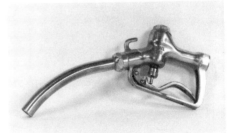

Gasoline Pump Nozzle. 14" l. Brass. Very minor wear. Display 8½. **$10**

Gas Globes

"AllFire" Gas Globe. 13½" dia. Red ripple body. "The Security Oil Co./Wichita Kansas" is in white lettering. "Allfire" is red lettering. Red anchor on blue sky and blue and white waves background. Very minor chipping inside base. Display 9/Reverse 8½. **$1500**

"Atlantic/Polarine/Gasoline" Gas Globe. 15" dia. One piece milk glass chimney top. Blue lettering. "Atlantic" logo in center in blue. Rare item. Base chipped overall. Fading to lettering. Display 6+. **$1500**

"American Liberty/Regular" Gas Globe. 13½" dia. Milk glass lens. Blue ripple body. Blue and red lettering. Red, white, and blue bust of the Statue of Liberty. "Property of American Liberty Oil Company" is at bottom. Minor chipping to inside of rim at base. Display 9/Reverse 9. **$1500**

"Bell" Gas Globe. 13½" dia. Rippled body. Metal base. Orange body. "Bell" is in blue lettering shadowed in white. Blue bell has blue derrick on white background. Rust to metal base. Minor scratches to reverse side. Display 8/Reverse 7. **$1400**

"Ben Franklin/Premium Regular" Gas Globe. 13½" dia. White rippled body. Milk glass lenses. Red and white lettering. Picture of Ben Franklin is dark blue. Red border around sides and top. Fantastic globe. Band has paint chips. Minor paint chipping at base. Display 9/Reverse 9. **$1700**

"Champlin/Gasoline" Gas Globe. 13½" dia. Milk glass body. Blue and white lettering. "Use Champlin Oils" logo in the center in red, white, and blue. Minor soiling, minor chipping. Display 7/Reverse 7. **$300**

"Champlin/Ethyl/Gasoline" Gas Globe. 13½" dia. Three-piece glass. Blue lettering on white background. Black and yellow. "Ethyl" logo. Ethyl Gasoline/Corporation/New York, U.S.A. Crack at base. Display 8/Reverse 8. **$350**

"Champlin/Presto/Gasoline" Gas Globe. 13½" dia. Glass body. Blue and red letters on white background. Blue border. Minor soiling at base. Display 8½/Reverse 8½. **$200**

"Cities Service/Koolmotor" Gas Globe. 15″ h. Clover leaf shaped glass. Three-piece. Black and yellow-gold lettering. Black clover outline around edge and in center. Black outlined triangle in center of clover. Cracked on reverse side. Minor paint at the base. Soiling on reverse. Display 8½/Reverse 5. **$700**

"Cushing/Gasoline" Gas Globe. 13½″ dia. Three-piece glass body. Black lettering. Red and white logo. Soiling to lenses on reverse. Very minor green paint spots at base. Display 8/ Reverse 7. **$300**

"Conoco" Gas Globe. 13½″ dia. Plastic. Green body. Red, white, and green triangle logo. Red and white letters. "Reg. U.S. Pat. Off./Manufactured In The U.S.A." Soiling to plastic body. Very minor scratches to lenses. Display 8½/Reverse 8½. **$150**

"Dixie/Oils/Gasoline" Gas Globe. 15″ dia. Jeweled yellow metal band. Yellow background with red, white, and blue letters. Blue oval. "Power to Pass" appears in blue. Minor paint chipping to body. Display 9/Reverse 9. **$1700**

"Diamond" Gas Globe. 15″ dia. One-piece white milk glass. Red diamonds and red lettering. Minor fading to paint. Display 7½/Reverse 7½. **$500**

"D-X/Ethyl" Gas Globe. 13½″ dia. Three-piece glass body. Black, red, and white lettering. Red diamond in the background. "Lubricating Motor Fuel." Minor scratching on reverse. Display 9/ Reverse 8. **$350**

"Diamond/D-X" Gas Globe. 13½″ dia. Three-piece milk glass body. "Lubricating Motor Fuel." Black and white lettering. Red diamond in the background. Red paint to base. Chipping to rim. Display 8/Reverse 8. **$100**

"Esso" Gas Globe. 15″ dia. Blue metal band. "Esso" is in blue script lettering. Milk glass lenses. Red border. New band. Display 9/Reverse 9. **$300**

"Globe/Gasoline" Gas Globe. 13½" dia. Three-piece glass body. Blue and white globe showing North and South America with blue and white letters. Red border. Metal band around lens is paint chipped overall. Minor chipping at base to lenses. Display 8½. **$700**

"Hudson Oil Co./Transport Gasoline" Gas Globe. 13½" dia. Three-piece glass globe milk glass. Gray and white tanker truck with an orange sun in the background. Black and orange lettering. Fine example of a globe. Numerous scratches on lenses. Minor chipping inside of rim. Display 8/Reverse 7. **$1000**

"Haney's/Gasoline" Gas Globe. 15" dia. Red metal band. Milk glass lenses. Blue and red lettering. Red "H" with blue arrow in the center of globe. "Independent/Dependable." Label on bottom of body says "The Cincinnati/Advertising Products Co./Cincinnati, Ohio U.S.A." Band has paint loss. Display 9/Reverse 9. **$500**

"Illinois Oil Co./Torpedo/Gasoline" Gas Globe. 15" dia. Metal body. Green and red. Red lettering. Black and white torpedo in the center. Very scarce. Paint chipping and rust to body and base. Minor scratches to both sides. Display 7/Reverse 6½. **$600**

"Indian/Gas" Gas Globe. 13½" dia. Three-piece glass. Blue lettering. Red dot in center. Metal base. Crack at top of body. Display 9/Reverse 8½. **$300**

"Mobilgas" Gas Globe. 16½" dia. Red metal body. Milk glass lenses. Black lettering. Red pegasus horse with white highlights. Minor paint chipping to body. Minor scratches to lenses. Display 8/Reverse 8. **$400**

"Marathon" Gas Globe. 15" dia. Red metal body. Milk glass lenses. "Marathon" is green lettering outlined in black. Orange marathon runner. Very minor rust to metal body. Lenses have very minor scratches. Display 8/Reverse 8. **$800**

"NevrNox/Diamond/Gasolene/Product" Gas Globe. 15" dia. One piece milk glass. Red, black, and white lettering. Base is cracked and chipped. Display 8. **$1000**

"Phillips/66/Ethyl" Gas Globe. 13½" dia. Plastic body. Creme. Body is original. White milk glass lenses. "Ethyl" is in black lettering on an orange background. Emblem is black and orange. Body is heavily soiled. Display 9/Reverse 9. **$300**

"Rose Bud/Power/Penn/Gasoline" Gas Globe. 13½" dia. Three-piece glass. Red and black lettering. Red rose with green leaves in the center. White highlights. Black border. Red paint at base of body. Display 9/Reverse 9. **$700**

"Rock Island/AntiKnock Gasoline" Gas Globe. 15" dia. Metal body. Red and white lettering on a blue ring outlined in red. Metal band has paint on it at the top and lenses. Rust to body. Body may be repainted. Display 8/Reverse 6½. **$300**

"Sinclair/Gasoline" Gas Globe. 13½" dia. One piece milk glass with bars. Green with white lettering. Chip out of base. Fading and paint loss overall. Display 6/Reverse 6. **$600**

"Skelly/Aromax" Gas Globe. 13½" dia. Three-piece glass. Metal base. Blue lettering. "Ethyl" logo is in black and yellow on red circle. "Ethyl Gasoline/Corporation/New York, U.S.A." Base rusty. Display 8½/Reverse 8½. **$300**

"Sovereign/SS" Gas Globe. 13½" dia. Yellow ripple glass body. Maroon lettering. "SS" is yellow on maroon shield. Minor scratches to lenses. Chipping to inside of rim. Display 8/Reverse 8. **$800**

"Southern/Marketer, Inc." Gas Globe. 13½" dia. Glass body. Metal base. State of Indiana with blue stream, green trees, brown rocks, and shoreline. Very nice example of a globe. Display 9/Reverse 9. **$900**

"Sunray/Gasoline" Gas Globe. 13⅓" dia. Orange ripple glass body. Black lettering. Yellow sunrays. Orange and green background. Body is cracked at the bottom overall. Display 9/Reverse 9. **$900**

"Texaco/Ethyl" Gas Globe. 15″ dia. One piece milk glass. "Texaco/Ethyl" in black embossed letters. Logo in the center has a red star with green "T" outlined in an embossed black border. Threaded base. Logo has minor fading. Missing metal band on base. Display 8/Reverse 8. **$1000**

"Tydol" Gas Globe. Ca 1935–1945. 14″ dia. Lens is white with orange and black border. "Tydol" is in black letters. Casing is metal painted black. Reverse side cracked overall in 3 places. Display 8/Reverse 5. **$150**

Pump Plates

"Atlantic" Pump Sign. 7″ h. 13″ w. Red and white with blue lettering. Very minor chipping to one corner and rust around edges. Display 8. **$25**

"Conoco" Pump Sign. 7½″ h. 8½″ w. Porcelain. Red and white triangle upside down. "Conoco" is white over a red rectangle across center of triangle. Minor scratches, chipping around holes. Display 8½. **$100**

"Fire-Chief/Gasoline" Pump Sign. 1942. 12″ h. 8″ w. Porcelain. Rare small size. White background. "Fire-Chief" is in red letters outlined in black. Red and white racing stripes. "Gasoline" is in black. White, red, and gold hat with black accents. "Texaco" logo left center. Chipping around edges and is soiled. Display 8. **$100**

"Indian Gasoline" Rounded Pump Sign. 1940. 18″ h. 12″ w. Porcelain. Green and blue with white and green lettering. Teepees design of red, white, black, and yellow at top. "Made in U.S.A./9-40." Chipping at bottom and left side edge and rust to edge. Display 8. **$150**

"Little Giant" Pump Sign. 10½″ dia. Porcelain. Round white background. Picture of giant man standing against the world with open arms. Man is white with black accents, red world with black. "Little Giant" is black. Touched up spot on right leg and right bottom edge, chipping upper left edge. Display 8. **$150**

"Metro" Die Cut Pump Plate. 13″ h. 12½″ w. Porcelain. White with green lettering. Red horse outlined in green, highlighted in white. "Texlite Dallas." Very Scarce. Chipping to edge by "M" in "Metro" and above mounting hole at top right. Display 8 +. **$500**

"Sea Chief" Embossed Pump Sign. 10" h. 15" w. Painted tin. Gold and white background. Black lettering. Red and green "Texaco" logo at bottom center. Minor scratches. Display 8. **$150**

"Mobiloil" Die Cut Pump Plate. 1946. 12" h. 12" w. Blue lettering with red horse outlined in blue, highlighted in white. White background with blue border. Minor yellow spotting. Display 8½. **$300**

"100% Pure Pennsylvania Oil" Die Cut Pump Sign. 9¾" h. 12" w. Porcelain. Golden yellow and black background and lettering. Doublesided. Sun fading and edge chipping. Display 6½/Reverse 6½. **$150**

"Sky Chief" Pump Sign. 1942. 12" h. 8" w. Porcelain. Rare size. "Sky Chief" is red lettered on white background over green. "Texaco" logo at bottom left. "Gasoline" is white on black. Red wing outlined in black. Chipping around edges, surface scratches, scuffing. Display 8. **$100**

"Socony/Motor/Oil" Pump Sign. 15″ h. 15″ w. Porcelain. Blue lettering on a white background bordered in red and blue. Chipping to mounting holes and minor scratches. Display 7½. **$75**

"Blue Sunoco/200" Pump Plate. 21″ h. 15″ w. Porcelain. Yellow with blue and yellow lettering. Red arrow. Scratching to very edge. Display 8½. **$100**

Left: "Sterling Gasoline" Pump Sign. 10″ h. 11½″ w. Porcelain. Yellow and white with black lettering. Red "L" design in center. "A Quaker State Product" at bottom. Display 9. **$250**; Right: "Sterling Gasoline" Pump Sign. 9″ h. 11½″ w. Porcelain. Yellow and white with black lettering. Black and yellow "Ethyl" logo in center. Display 9. **$200**

"Blue Sunoco" Pump Sign. 8″ h. 12″ w. Porcelain. Yellow with blue lettering. Scratching to edges. Display 8. **$75**

"Blue Sunoco" Porcelain Pump Sign. 22″ h. 19″ w. Porcelain. Blue with yellow diamond. Red arrow. Blue lettering. Edge rust. Display 8½. **$75**

"Texaco" Round Porcelain Pump Sign. 15″ dia. White with black border. Red star. Green "T." "Texaco" in black. Chips to edges and overall. Display 5+. **$200**

"Tydol/Flying/A" Pump Sign. 9¾″ dia. Black lettering on a cream background. "A" is red with white wings outlined in black on green background. Red border around sign. Chipping around edges, surface scratches, some discoloring to red border. Display 8½. **$150**

CHAPTER 2

Pour It On:

Oil Cans of All Sizes

Oil cans are a favorite collectible because they come in a range of sizes and prices. For most collectors, graphics make an oil can desirable. Some of the oil cans depicted here date from as early as 1915. (Oil bottles are included in Chapters 3 and 5.) In the 1960s, gas stations, car dealers, and auto parts stores started selling oil in plastic containers, thereby making the oil can an even more coveted object of nostalgia. All cans are made of tin unless otherwise noted.

One-Quart Cans

Left: 1-qt "Air Race/Motor Oil." Ca 1935–1945. 5½" h. 4" dia. A yellow airplane angles upward on a creme background. A yellow band extends across the bottom. "Deep-Rock" is red with blue outline. "Deep Rock Oil Corporation" is at the bottom. Can has scratches at the top. Rust at the bottom of can covers some letters in the company name. This can has no top or bottom. Display 6. **$30**; *Center:* 1-qt "Hyvis/Motor Oil." Ca 1935–1945. 5½" h. 4" dia. The can is black with "Mileage Metered" in yellow script at the top. "Hyvis Motor Oil" is in white. There is a red symbol that spells out "Oil" in red. Bottom reads "Product Of/Hyvis Oils, Inc./Warren, Pennsylvania." Can has no top. Display 7½. **$30**; *Right:* 1-qt "Golden/Leaf/Motor Oil." Ca 1935–1945. 5½" h. 4" dia. The can is royal blue with golden yellow lettering and a golden yellow leaf in the middle. Display 7½. **$25**

1-qt "American/Coach Oil." Ca 1870–1890. 6¾" h. Triangular shaped. "Manufactured by/ Standard Oil Co./Cleveland, Ohio." This oil was used for lubricating axles of carriages, coaches, buggies, and cabs. This is a very early soldered tin oil can with graphic of stagecoach with horses. Possibly unique. Display 7. **$250**

Left: 1-qt "Bisonoil." Ca 1935–1945. 5½" h. 4" dia. A red and black bison stands at the top overlooking the word "Bisonoil" in white outlined in red. "The Bison Oil Products Co., Inc./ Buffalo, N.Y." is written across the bottom. The can has white background on top half and black on bottom half. This can has very few scratches, which are on the back. Front is mint. Display 9. **$85**; *Center:* 1-qt "Phillips/Trop-Artic/Motor Oil." Ca 1935–1945. 5½" h. 4" dia. Blue can with off white stripes and band around diameter of can. "Phillips" On orange and blue shield on off-white circle. "Trop-Artic" in script in blue outlined in off-white. Display 9 + . **$170**; *Right:* 1-qt "Penn-Bee/Motor Oil." Ca 1935–1945. 5½" h. 4" dia. There are two bees in a red circle above the word "Penn-Bee." Bees are black and yellow. There is a logo in lower left corner. "Thermoil Lubricants Corp., Elk City, Oklahoma" appears in red band at bottom. Display 8. **$140**

Left: 1-qt "20-W/Motor Oil." Ca 1935–1945. 5½" h. 4" dia. Can is blue with a yellow insert showing a snow graphic. "20-W" is blue with snow lying on top. "Motor Oil" is in white letters. "The Canfield Oil Company" is at bottom of can. Display 8½. **$45**; *Center:* 1-qt "National/En-Ar-Co/Motor Oil." Ca 1935–1945. 5½" h. 4" dia. Can has three colors as background. Creme is the top color, next is turquoise, then red. In turquoise, there is a young boy holding a chalkboard with the "National" logo. Display 9. **$35**; *Right:* 1-qt "Sinclair/Pennsylvania/Motor Oil." Ca 1935–1945. 5½" h. 4" dia. Can is red with a black dinosaur at the bottom. "Sinclair" is in white with black shadowing. "Pennsylvania/Motor Oil" is in red surrounded by a moon shape in white. "Mellowed/100 Million Years" at bottom below dinosaur. Display 8. **$25**

Left: 1-qt "H D/Motor Oil." Ca 1935–1945. 5½" h. 4" dia. Two bands of red and one of white color this can. The letters "H D" are in white with black shadowing. A little picture of Drake Well with the words "Colonel Drake" is in the center of these letters. Display 8. **$20**; *Center:* 1-qt "Phillips/66/Aviation/ Engine Oil." Ca 1935–1945. 5½" h. 4" dia. Light blue with horizontal stripes of silver around can. Graphics of various airplanes on top of band of silver. Black-winged "Phillips/66" logo at center of can is bright orange, black, and silver. Display 8 +. **$40**; *Right:* 1-qt "Fleet-Wing/Motor Oil." Ca 1935–1945. 5½" h. 4" dia. A bird colored in orange is in flight on a creme background. "Certified" is written above the bird. "Fleet-Wing/Motor Oil" is written in creme and shadowed in blue on an orange background. Some rust on back seam. Display 7½. **$25**

Left: 1-qt "Double/Eagle/Motor Oil." Ca 1935–1945. 5½" h. 4" dia. A two-headed eagle is holding a ribbon that says "Guards Your Motor." Eagle has a red dot behind it on a dark blue background. "Double/Eagle/Motor Oil" is in silver letters. A red band goes across top and bottom of can. Band on bottom says "Double Eagle Lubricants, Inc./Oklahoma City, Okla." Display 9. **$20**; *Center:* 1-qt "Noco/ Motor Oil." Ca 1935–1945. 5½" h. 4" dia. Can is blue with a Viking in the center holding a shield with "The Nourse Brands" logo. All lettering is creme. "Nourse Oil Co. Kansas City, Mo." is at the bottom. Display 9. **$10**; *Right:* 1-qt "Cruiser/Motor/Oil." Ca 1935–1945. 5½" h. 4" dia. Can shows a scene of a cruise ship on water overlaying a black diamond. "Cruiser" is in bold black. "100% Pure/Pennsylvania/Motor/Oil" is in yellow and black. Display 8. **$140**

Left: 1-qt "Freedom/Perfect/Motor Oil." Ca 1935–1945. 5½" h. 4" dia. Can has a bulldog at the top. All lettering is in blue with a yellow background bordered in blue. "The/Freedom Oil Works Co./Freedom, PA." is at the bottom. Display 8½. **$100**; *Center:* 1-qt "Heart/O'/Pennsylvania." Ca 1935–1945. 5½" h. 4" dia. Can has "Heart/O'/Pennsylvania" at the top overlaid on a red heart. Toward bottom, there is a navy blue band saying "100% Pure/Pennsylvania/Motor Oil." "Pennsylvania" is in red; the rest is colored in silver. Silver paint is faded. Display 8. **$45**; *Right:* 1-qt "Quaker/City/Motor Oil." Ca 1935–1945. 5½" h. 4" dia. Can shows a scene of a city in navy blue with a creme background. "Quaker/City" is also in navy blue. At the bottom is orange with text. There are two symbols at the bottom of the can. Can has minor scratches toward the bottom. Can has no top. Display 7½. **$70**

Left: 1-qt "Harris/Oils" Ca 1935–1945. 5½" h. 4" dia. Yellow can pictures an oil barrel. "Harris/America's/Leading Lubricants" is in yellow gold. "Oils" is written across the barrel. A red and black band runs across the top and bottom of can. Display 9. **$120**; *Center:* 1-qt "Nourse/Motor Oil." Ca 1935–1945. 5½" h. 4" dia. Shows a Viking on a hill holding the "Nourse Brands" logo. In background is a Viking ship and Vikings. Lettering is on a black background. Bottom says "Nourse Oil Co., Kansas City, Mo. U.S.A." Background of Viking is green and white. A small dent on side. Display 8½. **$20**; *Right:* 1-qt "Pennzoil/Motor Oil." Ca 1935–1945. ½" h. 4" dia. A yellow can with red and black borders. Shows three owls perched on a "Pennzoil" logo. Lettering is black. "Pennzoil" is overlaid on a red bell. Display 7. **$55**

Left: 1-qt "Johnson/Motor/Oil." Ca 1935–1945. 5½" h. 4" dia. At top there is a logo of an hourglass with wings. The wings say "Time Tells." "Johnson" is in creme with a black background. "Motor/Oil" is in black with a creme border on an orange background. Towards bottom of can says "Johnson Oil Refining Co./Chicago, Ill." Can is creme. Display 8. **$120**; *Center:* 1-qt "Ace High/Motor Oil." Ca 1935–1945. 5½" h. 4" dia. On the front is a blue and white sunburst with an early touring car and a plane in the clouds inside it. "Ace High" is above the clouds in white with a red outline. Three logos are at the bottom of the can. The sunburst is overlaying a red background. There is no bottom to this can. Very little fading. Display 8. **$135**; *Right:* 1-qt "Genuine/Oil." Ca 1935–1945. 5½" h. 4" dia. Can is orange with a black symbol. "Harley-Davidson/Motor/Cycles" logo is in center of can. "Harley-Davidson Motor Co./Milwaukee/U.S.A." is written toward the bottom. Display 9. **$40**

Left: 1-qt "Lion Head/Motor Oil." Ca 1935–1945. 5½" h. 4" dia. On a banner in the center of the can is a lion head in red and yellow with black highlights. "Monarch of Oil" is at the top of can. The can has a yellow border with a red background. This can has very little wear on it. The luster is faded a bit. Display 9. **$35**; *Center:* 1-qt "Oilzum/Motor Oil." Ca 1935–1945. 5½" h. 4" dia. This can is orange with a man in an orange hat that reads "Oilzum." "Motor Oil" is in black at the bottom of can. The man is in orange and black on a white and orange background. Reverse side says "The White & Bagley Co./ Worcester, Mass. U.S.A." Can has no top. Can has minor dents and scratches. Display 7. **$90**; *Right:* 1-qt "Indian/Premium/Motorcycle Oil." Ca 1935–1945. 5½" h. 4" dia. Two American Indians with a white circle around them are on both sides of "Indian" in yellow on a band across the top. "Premium" is written in red on an explosion of white on a yellow background. "Indian Motorcycle Company/ Springfield, Massachusetts, U.S.A." is written across a red band at the bottom. Display 7½. **$100**

32

Left: 1-qt "Maxoil" Ca 1935–1945. 5½" h. 4" dia. White can with blue and red bands top and bottom. "Maxoil" in red across graphic of early car. "Special" in script is blue over white "Cylinder/Lubricant" in block letters that are red over white. Display 9 +. **$55**; *Center:* 1-qt "Arrow/Lubricant." Ca 1935–1945. 5½" h. 4" dia. Blue and white/gray stripes cover this can with stripes turning to arrow shapes at top and bottom of can. A "100% Pure Pennsylvania" logo is at the bottom of the oval shape. "Arrow/Lubricant" is in blue with white/gray shadowing. Luster is faded. Display 8. **$50**; *Right:* 1-qt "Superol/Motor Oil." Ca 1935–1945. 5½" h. 4" dia. A yellow can with a red aircraft angled upward. A red dot with a little black is above "ol" at top of can. Band at bottom and rectangle above plane are black. "Rugged/ Quality" is written towards bottom left. Display 8. **$20**

Left: 1-qt "Mohawk/Chieftain/Motor Oil." Ca 1935–1945. 5½" h. 4" dia. There is a Mohawk Indian at the bottom with a red and white feather surrounded by a red circle on a royal blue background. Upper half is white with the words "Mohawk/Motor Oil" in royal blue. "Chieftain" is in a bright red. "Mohawk Refining Corp. Newark 5, N.J. U.S.A." is at the bottom. This can has a very small dent at the bottom; otherwise mint. Display 9. **$100**; *Center:* 1-qt "Aero/Mobiloil." Ca 1935–1945. 5½" h. 4" dia. Can is white with a gray band around the center with the words "gray band" in white. A gargoyle and the word "Gargoyle" appear in red at the top center. "Make The Chart Your Guide" is in black above the gargoyle. "Socony-Vacuum Oil Company/Made in U.S.A." is written at the bottom. Display 8. **$80**; *Right:* 1-qt "Penntroleum/Motor Oil." Ca 1935–1945. 5½" h. 4" dia. A motorboat with an American flag is on a lake under a bridge that has touring cars and people on it. In the air are planes. Two logos are at the lower corners. Motorboat is red. Planes, people, and cars are blue. "Cato Oil and Grease Company/Oklahoma City, Oklahoma" is written at the bottom. Display 8. **$150**

Left: 1-qt "Moore's/C-75/Motor/Oil." Ca 1935–1945. 5½" h. 4" dia. A "Moore' symbol rests under the word "Moore's" at the top on a yellow background. A band of red runs across the center with "C-75" in a yellow oval. "Motor/Oil" is in a black band around the bottom. Minor scratches and dents on can. Display 7. **$15**; *Center:* 1-qt "Thompson/Products/Aerotype/Break-In/Motor Oil." Ca 1935–1945. 5½" h. 4" dia. Yellow can has horizontal black pinstripes all the way around it. Graphic of prop airplane appears in yellow and black. "Thompson Products" in yellow on a black circle center of can. "Thompson Products, Inc./Cleveland, Ohio U.S.A." Display 9. **$80**; *Right:* 1-qt "Mother Penn/Motor Oil." Ca 1935–1945. 5½" h. 4" dia. White can has picture of Mother Penn at top center with date "1879" on both sides of her. The words "Mother Penn" are blue shadowed in red over white. "Motor Oil" is red shadowed in blue over white. "Dryer Clark and Dryer Oil Co./Oklahoma City, Okla." appears at bottom of can. Minor scuffs on top edge of can. Display 9++. **$55**

Left: 1-qt "Para-Field/Motor Oil." Ca 1935–1945. 5½" h. 4" dia. Depicts an early oil well with a yellow background. "Para-Field" is in red with a black shadowing. "Definitely Superior Lubrication" appears at the bottom. Display 7. **$110**; *Center:* 1-qt 'Mobiloil/"BB".' Ca 1935–1945. 5½" h. 4" dia. A black and red graphic design is at top. Below is a picture of a gargoyle in red and the word "Gargoyle" in red and black. Background is creme. Some discoloring on back, but condition is otherwise excellent. A very desirable can. No top. Display 8½. **$80**; *Right:* 1-qt "Pennzoil/Motor Oil." Ca 1935–1945. 5½" h. 4" dia. A red bell on a yellow background has "Pennzoil" in black letters overlaying it. A black and red band runs across the bottom. Graphic of an airplane is on top half. Display 8. **$60**

Left: 1-qt Penguin Motor Oil. Ca 1935–1945. 5½" h. Blue can with a penguin pictured in center. "Penguin" is red outlined in blue on a white band. Red band across bottom says "A H. Grade Eastern Oil." Display 7. **$120**; *Center:* 1-qt Pennzoil Motor Oil. Ca 1935–1945. 5½" h. Yellow can with Pennzoil logo of red bell is pictured at bottom. "Main Liner" airplane is pictured. "Be Oil Wise" Owls are at bottom. "Filled and Sealed by/Pennzoil Company/Refineries: Oil City, PA." appears on back. Display 8. **$45**; *Right:* 1-qt Sinclair Motor Oil. Ca 1936–1945. 5½" h. Red can with a black dinosaur behind a white sign with "Pennsylvania/Motor Oil" in black lettering on it. "Sinclair" is white shadowed in black. "Mellowed 100/Million Years" is white at bottom. "Sinclair Refining Company Inc./New York, N.Y." Display 8. **$175**

Left: 1-qt "H D/Motor Oil." Ca 1950s. 5½" h. 4" dia. "H D" are in bright red letters. A Penn Drake symbol is at the top center with a picture of Drake Well and words "Penn Drake". Can is white with a red band toward bottom and a yellow band at bottom. This was a display can. Display 9. **$30**; *Center:* 1-qt "Phillips/66/Motor Oil." Ca 1935–1945. 5½" h. 4" dia. Can is maroon with creme stripes. Phillips symbol is at top in red and black with creme circle under symbol. "Premium" is in black letters. "Motor Oil" is creme with a black outline. Display 9. **$30**; *Right:* 1-qt "Mobiloil." Ca 1935–1945. 5½" h. 4" dia. Can has a red horse with wings at top. "Mobiloil" is in dark blue. There is a red stripe at the bottom. Display 8. **$30**

Left: 1-qt "Penn/Drake/Motor Oil." Ca 1935–1945. 5½" h. 4" dia. Can is red with a graphic design of Drake Well and the words "Penn/Drake" under. Across the top it reads "The Original Drake Well, 1859." On the bottom it reads "Motor Oil." All lettering is white. Display 8. **$35**; *Center:* 1-qt "Penn/ Champ/Motor Oil." Ca 1935–1945. 5½" h. 4" dia. A gold can with dark and light diamond shapes as a background with a red band bordered in white toward the bottom. A black rectangle at top of band has "10W-20W-30" written on it. A red rectangle above band has "Penn/Champ" written across it. Rust and scratches are toward bottom of can. Display 7. **$10**; *Right:* 1-qt "Kendall/The/2000 Mile/Oil." Ca 1935–1945. 5½" h. 4" dia. Red can with off-white oval that has gray graphic of right hand depicting victory sign at top. "Kendall/The/2000 Mile/Oil" is in red outlined in black. Graphics of a plane, car, boat, truck, and bus on black band at bottom of can. Display 8. **$25**

Left: 1-qt "Wil-Flo/Motor/Oil." Ca 1935–1945. 5½" h. 4" dia. Can shows a snow scene with pine trees covered in snow on a dark blue background. "At/30 Degrees/Below" is written on the snow. Red bands go across the top and bottom of can. Some rust on back seam. Display 7. **$65**; *Center:* 1-qt "Golden/Shell/Motor Oil." Ca 1935–1945. 5½" h. 4" dia. The shell is red with orange highlights. "Golden/Shell" is creme with a red outline and orange shadowing. "Motor Oil" is in red. The can has an orange background with red stripes across both top and bottom. Some minor dents. Display 8. **$85**; *Right:* 1-qt "Invader/Motor/Oil." Ca 1950s. 5½" h. 4" dia. This was used as a display can. A knight with his armor is riding a horse and carrying a shield. "Invader" appears in black with yellow and red outlining. Can is bright yellow with a black band across bottom with "Chas. F. Kellom and Co., Inc./ Philadelphia, PA. 19136" written in it. Display 9. **$15**

1-qt "Valvoline Oil Company." Ca 1873–1881. 3½" h. Reads "Valvoline Oil Company/New York, U.S.A." Valvoline trademark is in center. All lettering is black on a green background. Display 7. **$275**

Five-Quart Cans

5-qt "Aero/Mobiloil." Ca 1935–1945. 9½" h. 6½" dia. A creme colored tin with a red band across the center with the words "Red/Band" in creme. A red gargoyle is at the top. The word "Gargoyle" is in black and red. Can has no top. Display 7. **$100**

5-qt "Freedom/Perfect/Motor Oil" Ca 1935–1945. 9½" h. 6½" dia. A blue can with a yellow emblem across the front. A bulldog is at the top in blue and white with "The Watchdog of Your Motor." All lettering is in blue. "Freedom Oil Company/Freedom, PA." is at the bottom. Can has no top. Display 7½. **$80**

5-qt "Gulflube/Motor Oil." Ca 1935–1945. 9½"
h. 6½" dia. "Gulf" is written in blue with white
and blue shadowing on an orange background
encircled in blue and white. "Gulflube/Motor Oil"
is at the top on a blue strip. Lettering is white.
Can has no top. Display 8. **$50**

5-qt "Harris/Oils." Ca 1935–1945. 9½" h. 6½"
dia. Can shows a picture of a wooden oil barrel
with the word "Oils" in white outlined in black.
End of barrel reads "Harris/America/Leading/
Lubricants" in yellow over black. Can has no
top. Display 7. **$75**

5-qt "Invader/Motor Oil." Ca 1935–1945. 9½" h. 6½" dia. A yellow can with a black band across the bottom. Can shows a knight in armour on a horse. "Chas. F. Kellom and Co Inc./Philadelphia" is at bottom. "Invader/Motor Oil" is black with white border. Display 8. **$75**

5-qt "Kendall/The/2000 Mile/Oil." Ca 1935–1945. 9½" h. 6½" dia. A red can with a black band across the bottom picturing a plane, car, boat, and bus. "Kendall/The/2000 Mile/Oil" is red outlined in black. A right hand making the victory sign is toward top on a creme oval shaped background. Can has no top. Display 7½. **$40**

5-qt "Mobiloil." Ca 1935–1945. 9½" h. 6½" dia. A creme colored can with a red gargoyle at the top. "Gargoyle" is black and red. A red band around the bottom reads "Socony-Vacuum Oil Company Inc./Made in U.S.A." The Mobiloil symbol is at the bottom. Display 8. **$90**

5-qt "Pennzoil" Motor Oil. Ca 1935–1945. 9½" h. 6½" dia. A yellow can with three owls pictured and "Be Oil Wise" written at bottom left Pennzoil logo is near bottom. Bell behind "Pennzoil" is red. Quote from "J.A. Herlihy, Director of Engineering, United Airlines" appears underneath an airplane on top half of can. Can has no top. Display 7½. **$90**

5-qt "Tru-Penn" Motor Oil. Ca 1935–1945. 9½"
h. 6½" dia. A green tin with "Tru-Penn" in black
outlined in white. "The Oilier Oil" is in decorative
script. "American/Lubricants/Incorporated/Buf-
falo, N.Y." is at the bottom. An American Lubricants logo is behind at the bottom. Can has no
top. Display 7. **$130**

Half-Gallon Cans

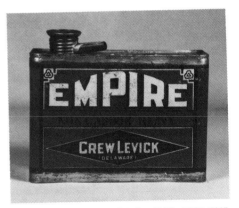

½-gal "Conoco/Harvester/Oil." Ca 1915–1925.
6½" h. 9½" w. Can has a minuteman standing
on right side. "Conoco" is in blue lettering with a
yellow shadow. "Harvester/Oil" and "Continental Oil Company" is in blue lettering on a white
background. Display side has a minor dent. Reverse side has dents and wrinkles. Display 8/
Reverse 7½. **$650**

½-gal "Empire" Motor Oil. Ca 1915–1925. 6¼"
h. 9½" w. "Crew Levick/Delaware" in white lettering in a black diamond with a red background.
Empire in white bold lettering in black shadowing at top of can. Display 9/Reverse 9. **$35**

½-gal "Lesh's/Arkoline/Products." Ca 1915–
1925. 6½″ h. 9½″ w. "Lesh's/Arkoline/Products"
is in red with a black border in center of can.
Rest of lettering is in black. "National Oil Co./
Arkansas City, Kansas." is at the bottom. Display 8 + . **$35**

½-gal "Red Top/Motor Oil." Ca 1917. 6¼″ h.
Can has a red spinning top in center and a red
touring car on a road beneath the spinning top.
"Take A Spin With" is in green and "Red Top" is
in red. "Motor Oil/Topp Oil" and "Supply Co./
370 E. Water St. Milwaukee" are in yellow on a
green background. Display 7½. **$300**

½-gal "Palacine/Palacine Oil Co." Ca 1917. 6″
h. 9½″ w. Can has white background with a red
border. "Palacine" is over a red barrel that is in
center of the design. "General Office/Ardmore,
Okla." is at the bottom of can. Display 9/Re-
verse 9. **$145**

½-gal "Richlube/Motor Oil." Ca 1925–1931.
6¼″ h. "Richlube" is in black with a light blue
shadow at top of can. "Richfield's/Partner in
Power" are at top and bottom of background in
yellow. "Richfield Oil Corp./ of New York/Gen-
eral Office New York" is written at bottom of can.
Display 7/Reverse 6. **$150**

½-gal "Pennant" Motor Oil. Ca 1915–1925.
6¼″ h. "The/Wonder Lubricant/for/Fords/Pierce
Petroleum Corporation" in yellow lettering with
black outlining. Pennant over a black circle
outlined in yellow and black. "Pennant" is green
with black outlining. Display 9/Reverse 8½. **$70**

½-gal "Tagolene Skelly Oil Co." Ca 1922–1929. 6″ h. Blue and red background. Creme, yellow and blue lettering. A yellow tag is hanging off "G" in "Tagolene." "Skelly Oil Company/El Dorado, Kansas" also appears. Minor overall scratches and scuffing. Display 7. **$210**

One-Gallon Cans

1-gal "Cross-Country/Motor/Oil." Ca 1915–1925. 11″ h. Can is creme and orange. "Sears Roebuck and Company" in black outlined in creme towards bottom of can. Can shows early touring car in country scene halfway down can. "Cross-Country/Motor/Oil" is white lettering with black outline. Display 8/Reverse has text. **$100**

1-gal "En-Ar-Co/Motor/Oil." Ca 1915–1925. 11″ h. Drawing of a young boy holding a chalkboard with "En-Ar-Co/Petroleum Products" written across the board is at top. "The National Refining Co./Cleveland, Ohio" is in black lettering at bottom of can. Can is yellow with a black and white border. Display 6½/Reverse 6. **$75**

43

1-gal "Galenol/Motor Oil." Ca 1915–1925. 9½″
h. "100% Pure/Pennsylvania/Oil" logo is at center of can. "Galenol/Motor Oil" is red with black
shadowing on a yellow background. Some writing is scratched on the can. Display 8 + /Re-
verse 8 + . $65

1-gal Indian Motor Oil. Ca 1915–1930. 11″ h.
"Indian Oil" in red. Green can with Indian head
logo top center. "Valvoline Oil Company/New
York, U.S.A./For The/Indian Motorcycle Com-
pany/Springfield Mass." Very rare in this condition. Display 8/Reverse 8. $1000

1-gal "Independent Motor Oil." Ca 1915–1925.
10½″ h. Graphic of marching colonial army in
center in sepia. Bright golden yellow background. "Independent/Motor Oil" is green
outlined in black. "Independent Oil Co./Altoona,
PA." is written on a green band at bottom of can.
This can is not often found. Display 8½/Reverse
7½. $220

1-gal "Kendall/Motor Oil." Ca 1915–1925. 10¾″
h. Photo-like picture of Kendall Refining Co. in
center. "Kendall Refining Company/Bradford,
PA" in white lettering with black outlining. Can
has red background. Display 7/Reverse 8. $75

44

1-gal "Keystone/Penetrating/Oil." Ca 1915–1925. 9½" h. Lettering is in red and silver on a black background. "Keystone Lubricating Co./ Philadelphia, PA., U.S.A." is at bottom of can. Paint is faded and can is scratched. Displays 6½/Reverse is in text 6. **$30**

1-gal "Nourse/Motor Oil." Ca 1917. 10½" h. "Jack Nourse Oil Co., Kansas City and Omaha" is written at the bottom. A creme background with a Viking in center dressed in green and black. "Nourse/Motor Oil" in creme on a black background. Outer edge green. This is a very rare can. Reverse has two dents in center. Display 7½/Reverse 7½. **$650**

1-gal "Mona Motor/Oil." Ca 1915–1925. 10½" h. Early touring cars in rural area. "Mona Motor/ Oil" in white lettering with black outline on a medium blue background. Wonderful graphics of plane, boat, touring car, bicycle, trader, steam shovel in black in background. Very rare to find in this size. Display 8½/Reverse is text 7. **$750**

1-gal "Opaline Motor Oil." Ca 1916–1918. 11" h. "Sinclair Refining Company/Chicago" is at the bottom. Shows a race car with "Sinclair/ Sinco/Oils" on grill. Beige background. Green car and lettering. Stain at bottom. Small dent. Super can. Display 8/Reverse 8. **$800**

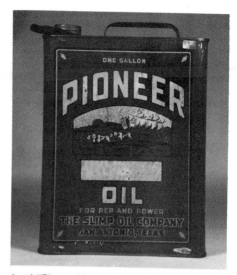

1-gal "Pennzoil" Motor Oil. Ca 1915–1925. 10¾″ h. "Pennzoil" is in black over a red bell in a yellow oval bordered in black and yellow. "Oil City, PA. Los Angeles, Cal." is written towards the bottom. A "Pennsylvania/Supreme/Quality" seal is at the bottom. Display 7½/Reverse 6½– 7. **$50**

1-gal "Pioneer/Oil." Ca 1917. 11″ h. "For Pep and Power" in gold lettering. "The Slimp Oil Company/San Antonio, Texas" in black lettering with gold outline near bottom of can. Has covered wagon with oxen in center of can. Can has red background. Display 7 + /Reverse 7 + . **$175**

1-gal "Pennzoil" Motor Oil. Ca 1915–1925. 11″ h. "Pennzoil" is written in black with silver border over a silver bell. Can has bright yellow background. "Refinery-Oil City, Pennsylvania" is written at the bottom. Display 7½–8/Reverse 6. **$170**

1-gal "Richlube/Motor Oil." Ca 1915–1925. 10¾″ h. "Richfield Oil Corp./of New York/General Office New York" at the bottom of can. "Richlube" in yellow shadowed in light blue with dark blue background. Bullseye pattern with "100% Pure/Pennsylvania/Oil" logo in center. Display 7½/Reverse is text 7½. **$350**

1-gal "Russolene/Brand/Motor Oil." Ca 1915–1925. 10½" h. Background is creme with a red border. "Russolene/Brand" is in blue with white outlining overlaying a red diamond. "Motor Oil" is in bright red lettering. "The Russian Oil Co./ Chicago, Ill." is in red at bottom of can. Display 8½/Reverse 8. **$110**

1-gal "Sliptivity." Ca 1920–1930. 12⅜" h. "C.C. Snowdon/Oil Refiner and Manufacturer." Features striking graphics of a train and steam ship. Blue on creme with sunburst of pale yellow. Blue lettering. "Sliptivity" is blue and gold. Lettering to one side is worn off. Other side is all there. Nice can. Rare. Display 8/Reverse 8. **$325**

1-gal "Tagolene" Motor Oil. Ca 1915–1925. 11" h. "Skelly Oil Company/El Dorado, Kansas" in blue on red band. "Tagolene" is embossed in yellow lettering. Can has blue background. A yellow tag is hanging from the "G." Display 7/ Reverse 6½. **$225**

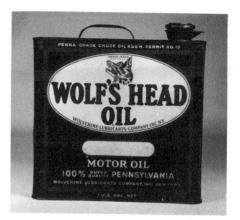

1-gal "Wolf's Head/Oil." Ca 1915–1925. 8¾" h. "Wolf's Head/Oil" logo over a creme oval bordered in orange. "Motor Cylinder/Heavy/Oil." Can has dark green background. "Wolverine Lubricants Company/New York" is at the bottom. Display 6½–7/Reverse 6. **$60**

1-gal "Wolf's Head/Oil." Ca 1915–1925. 9½" h. "Wolf's Head/Oil" is in red lettering with green outlining encircled in a creme oval with red outlining. Can has green background. "Wolverine Lubricants Company, Inc. New York" is written at the bottom. Reverse side has dent at lower left. Display 9+/Reverse 8. **$85**

Two-Gallon Cans

Left: 2-gal "Airflite/Motor Oil." Ca 1925–1945. 11½" h. 8½" w. A propeller plane is flying in the blue sky. The plane is shaded in reds. "100% Paraffine Base" is in blue. "Airflite" is white with red and black shadows. Display 8/Reverse 7½. **$150**; *Right:* 2-gal "Fleetwood/Motor/Oil." Ca 1925–1945. 11" h. 8½" w. Can shows a red propeller plane flying upward on a white background in a shape of a circle outlined in red, white, and blue. "Fleetwood" is written on a white banner-like stripe at the top. Can is dark blue. "Traymore Lubricants, New York" is at the bottom. Can has some very minor scratches. Display 8/Reverse 7. **$150**

Left: 2-gal "All/American/Motor Oil." Ca 1925–1945. 11½" h. 8½" w. Can has gold strip across top and bottom with a truck, car, and plane symbol. A picture of North America is in the center in gold outlined in creme and red on a creme background. Pennsylvania's shape is highlighted in red and outlined in creme. A "100% Pure" logo is in lower left corner. Display 8/Reverse 7½. **$65**; *Right:* 2-gal "Penn City/Motor/Oil." Ca 1925–1945. 11½" h. 8½" w. A Quaker in blue is symbol at the top in a circle of red. "Penn City/Motor/Oil" is blue outlined in white and blue. Can is blue. "Penn City-/National Oil Co./Phila., PA" is in blue at the bottom. Display 8/Reverse 7½. **$100**

Left: 2-gal "Archer/Lubricants." Ca 1925–1945. 11½" h. 8½" w. An American Indian shooting a bow on a tan background. "Archer" is red with black border and an arrow across it. "Archer Petroleum Corp., Omaha, Neb." is at the bottom. Display 8/Reverse 7½. **$20**; *Right:* 2-gal "Ocean/Liner/Motor Oil." Ca 1925–1945. 11½" h. 8½" w. An ocean liner on the water is symbol towards bottom of can. Colors are orange and blues. Can is orange with a blue band outlined in creme-colored waves. "Traymore Lubricants, New York." is at bottom. Some minor dents. Display 7½/Reverse 7. **$110**

Left: 2-gal "Around The World Motor Oil." Ca 1925–1945. 10½″ h. 8½″ w. Can is red and yellow with blue band at bottom saying "The Atlas Oil Co., Cleveland, Ohio." "Around The World" is yellow outlined in black. "Motor Oil" is white outlined in black. Can pictures a globe of blue and orange encircled by a ring on which early cars are driving. Display 7/Reverse 7. **$100**; *Right:* 2-gal "Strata/ Motor Oil." Ca 1925–1945. 11½″ h. 8½″ w. Can is brick red with a yellow propeller plane and yellow lettering. "Tiona Petroleum Co., Philadelphia, Penna. U.S.A." is written on a yellow stripe at the bottom. Display 8/Reverse 7. **$100**

Left: 2-gal "Defender/Motor Oil." Ca 1925–1945. 11¼″ h. 8½″ w. Dark blue can with sentry or defender overlooking an encampment of tents. Sentry is white with blue outline on a light red background. "Defender/Motor Oil" is white outlined in blue. "Pennsylvania/Petroleum Products Co./ Philadelphia, PA" in white at bottom center. Display 8/Reverse 7. **$20**; *Right:* 2-gal "Zeppelin/Motor Oil." Ca 1925–1945. 11½″ h. 8½″ w. A zeppelin is flying over the sea. Various shades of blue brushstrokes are used. A dark blue stripe is across the bottom bearing the name "Zeppelin/Motor Oil" in red outlined in white. Display 7/Reverse 6. **$195**

50

2-gal "Eagle/Motor Oil." Ca 1925–1945. 11¼" h. 7½" w. A black tin with a black eagle encircled by a black ring saying "Eagle Oil & Supply Co./ Boston, Mass." in white. All other lettering is black. This is a very rare can. Display 8. **$100**

Left: 2-gal "Green/Ray/Motor/Oil." Ca 1925–1945. 11½" h. 8½" w. Can is yellow with green graphics. A car is racing upward from "The/General Refining Co." logo. Lightning bolts go across the top and bottom of the can. Reverse side has minor dents. Display 8/Reverse 7½. **$300**; *Right:* 2-gal "Pennsyl-vania/Penn Pool" Ca 1925–1945. 11½" h. 8½" w. Can is dark orange at top, light orange at center, and black at bottom. Can shows an oil field with a hillside. Bottom says "Industrial Oil Corp., Warren, PA." in orange. Display 8/Reverse 6½–7. **$50**

Left: 2-gal "Lubrite/Motor Oil." Ca 1925–1945. 11½" h. 8½" w. A blue can with a red horse with wings outlined in light gray. "Lubrite/Motor Oil" is light gray. Two red stripes go across can, one at top and one toward bottom. Display 7½/Reverse 7½. **$45**; *Right:* 2-gal "Silver/Shell/Motor Oil." Ca 1925–1945. 11½" h. 8½" w. A red can with yellow lettering. A shell is symbol at the bottom in yellow with red highlights and "Shell" written in red. Display 8½/Reverse is text (no grade). **$25**

Left: 2-gal "Motor Oil." Ca 1925–1945. 10½" h. 8½" w. A red can with a yellow plate picturing a red aircraft. "Motor/Oil" is yellow. "Dependable Lubrication/For Your Motor" is in red at the bottom. Display 8/Reverse 8. **$15**; *Right:* 2-gal "Aero Eastern/Motor Oil." Ca 1925–1945. 11½" h. 8½" w. A black can with an orange stripe. The airplane is white outlined in orange. The lettering is white outlined in orange. "Christenson Oil Co., Portland, Ore." is at bottom of circle. Display 8/Reverse 7½. **$50**

Left: 2-gal "Mountain/State/Motor Oil." Ca 1925–1945. 11¼" h. 8½" w. Yellow, off-white, blue, and greens. "Mountain/State" in blue lettering over off-white and yellow. "Motor Oil" is off-white over blue. Display 8 +/Reverse 8. **$80**; *Right:* 2-gal "Penguin/Motor Oil." Ca 1925–1945. 11¼" h. 8½" w. Dark blue with white and red bands. Graphic of penguin in center of oval in light blue on a light red and white background. "Penguin" is in red outlined in blue on a white band. "Traymore Lubricants, New York" is at bottom of can. Display 8 +/Reverse 8. **$120**

Left: 2-gal "Penn/Airliner/Motor Oil." Ca 1925–1945. 11½" h. 8½" w. Can is off-white at top and green at bottom. An aircraft is flying through a circle shaped like a tire with the words "Penn/Airliner" in white. "Wright Oil Company/Jersey City, N.J." is written at the bottom. Display 7/Reverse 6½. **$130**; *Right:* 2-gal "Ocean Liner/Motor/Oil." Ca 1925–1945. 11½" h. 8½" w. An aircraft in white with red and blue markings is flying across this can. The can is blue with a white banner across the top saying "Ocean Liner" in red with a blue outline. "Traymore Lubricants, New York, N.Y." is at the bottom. Display 8/ Reverse 7. **$125**

Left: 2-gal "Pennsyline/Motor and Tractor Oils." Ca 1915–1925. 11¾" h. 9¼" w. Can is blue with center banner of red. "Staunch/As A Quaker" in white outlined in blue over red at bottom of banner. Quaker-type bust is at top of banner in blue and white with red lips. "Pennsyline/Motor and Tractor Oils" is white outlined in blue. A very early 2-gal. tin. Display 7/Reverse 6 + +. **$35**; *Right:* 2-gal "Red Bell/Motor Oil." Ca 1925–1945. 11¼" h. 8½" w. Blood red can with red bell in circle on silver background highlighted in blue. "Red Bell/Motor Oil" is silver outlined in blue. "The Sico Company/ Mount Joy, PA." in blue on sides. Display 8 + /Reverse 8. **$60**

Left: 2-gal "Primus/Motor Oil." Ca 1925–1945. 11½" h. 8½" w. Can is olive green, black, and gold, showing a race track with four cars racing. Shows a crowd of people in the stands. Display 8/Reverse 7½. **$900**; *Right:* 2-gal "Grand/Champion/Motor/Oil." Ca 1925–1945. 11½" h. 8½" w. Can shows a race track with three drivers in their cars waving. A checkered flag is waving. The colors on this can are bright, not faded at all. There are greens, reds, blue, yellow, white, and black. Display 8/Reverse 7½. **$175**

Left: 2-gal "Rocket/Motor/Oil." Ca 1925–1945. 11½" h. 8½" w. A red can with a rocket symbol in blue and red. "Rocket" is white with blue shadowing. "Motor/Oil" is white with red shadowing on a dark blue design. Display 8½/Reverse 8. **$65**; *Right:* 2-gal "Nourse/Brands" Motor Oil. Ca 1925–1945. 11½" h. 8½" w. A green and white checkered can with a Viking symbol holding "The/Nourse/Brands" logo shield. "Nourse Oil Co./Omaha, Nebraska" is at the bottom. Sides are green and white checkerboard. Some minor dents and scuffs. Display 7½/Reverse 6½. **$90**

Left: 2-gal "Sturdy/Motor/Oil." Ca 1925–1945. 11¼" h. 8½" w. A green strip is on lower half of can depicting a green tree with a circle in green and white and a banner saying "It Stands/The/Heat/It Withstands/The/Cold" in black letters. "Socony-Vacuum Oil Company, Inc./Made in U.S.A." is at the bottom. Top of can is white with a green stripe. Display 7/Reverse 7. **$45**; *Right:* 2-gal "Lord/Calvert/ Auto/Oil." Ca 1925–1945. 8½" h. 9½" w. A sunburst of white and orange is the background with the outline of a city at bottom. One man is on each side; they are tipping their hats. They are dressed in black, orange, and white. "Columbia/Petroleum Products Co./Philadelphia, PA." is at the bottom. All lettering is in white surrounded by black. Display 7/Reverse 7. **$90**

Left: 2-gal "Traffic/Motor Oil." Ca 1925–1945. 11½" h. 8½" w. A blue can with a traffic light in light blue and white. "Traffic" is white with blue shadowing. A white banner says "Motor Oil" in dark blue. "Gulf Oil Corporation/Gulf Refining Company" is at bottom. Minor dent on reverse side. Display 8½/ Reverse 7½. **$45**; *Right:* 2-gal "Continental Motor Oil." Ca 1935–1945. 10½" h. "Continental Motor Oil" is white outlined in blue. Can pictures a soldier in blue and white. Stars are white on blue background. "On Guard/To Protect/Your Motor" is red. "100% Pennsylvania/Heavy/S.A.E. 40/Continental Refining Co./Oil City, PA." is in blue. "100% Pure" symbol is in bottom corner. Can is white. Minor dents. Display 7½/Reverse 7½. **$100**

Left: 2-gal "Tulane/Motor/Oil." Ca 1925–1945. 11½" h. 8½" w. Background is red. There are early cars, trucks, and buses on a highway. Scenery is green. "Tulane" is white with green shadows. Bottom says "Will Keep Your Motor Fit." in white letters. Display 8/Reverse 7½. **$100**; *Right:* 2-gal "Road/Boss/Motor Oil." Ca 1925–1945. 11½" h. 8½" w. Can is creme and green. At bottom of can there is a country scene showing a tractor in the field and a car and truck on the road. Birds are in the sky. A farm is shown in the background. Picture is in light green. "John Pritzfaff Hardware Co./ Milwaukee, Wisconsin" is written at bottom. Display 8/Reverse 7. **$100**

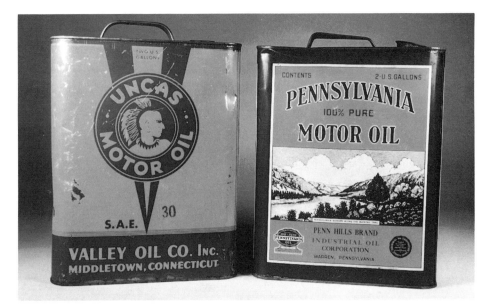

Left: 2-gal "Uncas/Motor Oil." Ca 1925–1945. 11½" h. 8½" w. An orange can with a green and orange symbol picturing an Indian. "Valley Oil Co. Inc./Middletown, Connecticut" is orange on a green strip. Display 6½/Reverse 6. **$80**; *Right:* 2-gal "Pennsylvania/Motor Oil" Ca 1925–1945. 11½" h. 8½" w. Can shows a picture of "Pennsylvania scenery along the Bucktail Trail." Colors in picture are blues, white, and golden yellow. Background is golden yellow with a creme and blue border. "Penn Hills Brand/Industrial Oil/Corporation/Warren, Pennsylvania" is at the bottom. Some minor dents. Display 7½/Reverse 7. **$95**

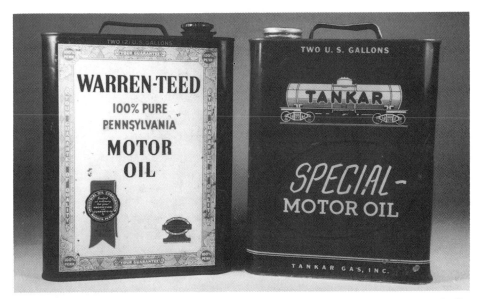

Left: 2-gal "Warren-Teed/Motor/Oil." Ca 1925–1945. 11½" h. 8½" w. A green border that looks like currency surrounds a white background with a ribbon in orange and black and a "100% Pure" logo at the bottom. Display 7½/Reverse 6. **$20**; *Right:* 2-gal "Tankar/Special/Motor/Oil." Ca 1925–1945. 11½" h. 8½" w. A background of red with a "Tankar" at the top. Car is black and beige. Letters are red with black border. "Special-/Motor Oil" is beige with black border. Display 7/Reverse 6½. **$45**

Left: 2-gal "Whippet Motor Oil." Ca 1925–1945. 10½″ h. Can is white with red lettering. Pictures a whippet dog. Top and bottom of can have red, white, and blue bands. "Pennsylvania Oil Company" is blue. Display 8/Reverse 8. **$210**; *Right:* 2-gal "Capitan Parlube Motor Oil." Ca 1925–1945. 10½″ h. Can shows car on a road with mountain in the background. "Capitan" is red and blue. "Parlube" is red. "Motor Oil/The Peak of Quality" is blue. "Parlube Oil Co./Beckett Bros., Holmes, PA." is white on red band at bottom. Scene is in colors of white, gray, pink, red, and navy. Display 8/Reverse 8. **$120**

Five-Gallon Cans

5-gal "Atlantic Motor Oil." Ca 1915–1925. 14½″ h. 9⅜″ w. Can is red with an "Atlantic Motor Oil" symbol on the front in blue and red. Top of can is embossed "The Atlantic Refining Company." Some minor scratches. Display 7/Reverse 7. **$40**

½-gal "Trop Artic/Auto Oil." Ca 1915–1925. 6¼" h. Can shows a scene of a touring car in the arctic and a touring car in the tropics. "Manhattan Oil Co." is at bottom. This can is in excellent condition and extremely desirable. Minor dents. Display 9 + . **$1000**

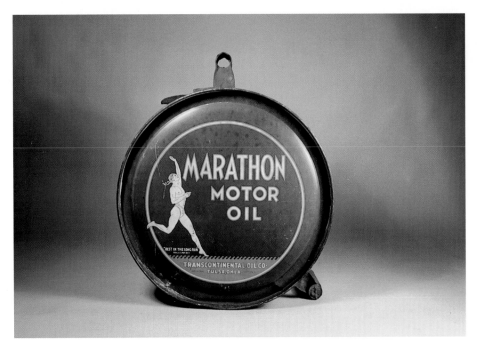

5-gal Easy-Pour. "Marathon/Motor/Oil." Ca 1915–1925. 16¾" h. 14¼" dia. A green tin with a marathon runner. "Marathon/Motor/Oil" is white with orange outline. "Transcontinental Oil Co./Tulsa, Okla" is at the bottom. Display 7½/Reverse 7. **$325**

1-gal "Golden/Shell/Auto Oil." Ca 1915–1925. 10½" h. Embossed logo of sea shell in center with gold and black recessed. "Golden/Shell/Auto Oil" in yellow outlined in black on orange background with overall black outline. This can is in excellent condition. One of the better Shell cans available. Minor scuffs. Display 9½/Reverse 8. **$800**

"Ryan's/Jet/Hi-Test" Gas Globe. Ca 1932–1940. 15″ dia. Glass lens and body. Red and blue lettering. Blue shield is outlined on lens background. Display 8. **$100**

"Red Hat/Gasoline" Gas Globe. 15″ dia. Metal body. Lettering is black. Red Hat with black band and white stars on one side. Reverse side has "Independent Oil Co. Seymour. MO." in black. Red stylized eagle on black upside down triangle. Lettering is white. Body has paint loss and rust overall. Independent lens faded and has paint loss. Display 9/Reverse 5. **$800**

Blue Grass Axle Grease Sign. 6½" h. 14" w. Painted tin. Orange and creme lettering. Indian Refining Corp logo in corner. Holes are punched inward. Was used on building to cover hole. Minor rust and soiling. Very few known. Display 7½. **$300**

Carter "CarBUREter" Light-Up Display. 27½" h. 13" w. Cast iron with milk glass globe. One piece. Red base. "Carter" on globe is black outlined in red; "Bure" in the center is black. Three name plates around bottom of base. One top bracket is missing. One bottom bracket is broken. Rust overall. Display 7½. **$800**

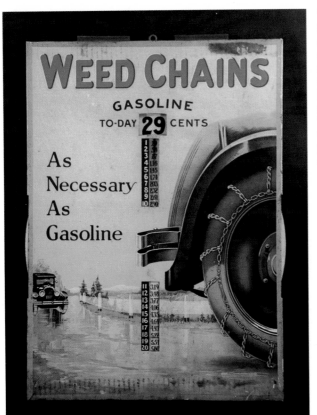

"Weed Chains" Price Display, 23″ h. 17″ w. Painted tin. Dial on side turns prices for the day. Back of early car with chains on right. Early car to left on road. Yellow, green, and blue colors; graphics are great. Blue and red lettering. "The American Art Works, Oshcochton, O." also appears. Rust and very minor denting. Display 7. **$800.**

½-gal "Mona Motor/Oil." Ca 1915–1925. 5¾″ h. 9½″ w. A touring car, tractor, bicycle, steam shovel, boat on a lake, and plane are pictured in black on the bottom half of this can. "Mona Motor/Oil/Monarch Mfg. Co." are white with black outlining. Can has ocean blue background. Display 9/Reverse (text) 9. **$250**

Michelin Air Compressor. Ca 1920–1930. 11″ h. Michelin Man sitting on cast metal housing of compressor. Brass metal plate on front of compressor reads ''R. TOUSSAINT & CO./WAGEOR & COU.FINHALL.'' Rubber handle. Compressor gauge on top. Includes hose. Extremely desirable piece. Very scarce. Paint has wear. Display 8+. **$1500**

5-qt ''Sinclair/Opaline/Motor Oil.'' Ca 1935–1945. 9½″ h. 6½″ dia. A green can with a red dinosaur at the bottom. ''Sinclair/Opaline/Motor Oil'' is written on a moon shape of creme. ''Mellowed/80 Million Years'' at the bottom. Can has no top. Display 7. **$60**

"Kelly/Tires" Flanged Sign. 24″ dia. Painted metal. "Kelly" curved over the top and "Tires" curved across bottom are black outlined in red. Picture of woman in early style red hat and coat driving in a green car. Left arm raised and waving. Double-sided. Wonderful sign. Wear to paint, overall fading, and rust. Display 7½/Reverse 7½. **$1900**

"Magnolia" Mobiloil Calendar. 1933. 23″ h. 14″ w. August, July and September shown. "Mobiloil" and "Mobilgas" logos at bottom and top. Car in mountain scene with plane flying over it are at right top of calendar. Ship on water in center. Watermark across half of calendar. Tear to "n" in "Magnolia." Display 6. **$50**

Wyeth Tires Curved Post Sign. 22″ h. 16″ w. Porcelain. Blue, white, and red colors. The word "Guaranteed" is in white at the top on the red border. "WYETH TIRES" letters are shadowed in white and red. Picture of the top half of a boy dressed in early automobile attire with hat and red goggles. He is inside a stack of three blue and white tires. The words "Ribbed/Wyco/Shield" appear—one on each tire. "WYETH HDW. & MFG. CO. ST. JOSEPH, MO., U.S.A." Minor scratches, chipping, and dent at top right. Chipping to porcelain above "T" and "H" in "WYETH." Chipping to porcelain on reverse side. Display 8½. **$1500**

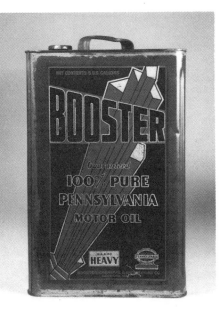

5-gal "Booster/Motor Oil." Ca 1915–1925. 14½" h. 9⅜" w. A black background surrounded in orange border. An orange graphic design is in the background. Letters are black with creme border. "Booster Chemical and Engineering Co./Baltimore, MD" is at the bottom. All sides are the same. Display 7½/Reverse 7½. **$125**

5-gal "En-Ar-Co/Motor/Oil." Ca 1915–1925. 14½" h. 9⅜" w. Yellow background picturing a young boy holding a chalkboard with "En-Ar-Co" logo. "National Refining Co./Cleveland, Ohio" is at the bottom. Display 7/Reverse 6. **$185**

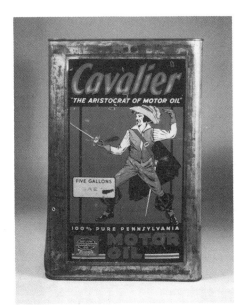

5-gal "Cavalier/Motor/Oil." Ca 1915–1925. 14½" h. 9⅜" w. An aristocrat is symbol in light purple. Purple bands go across top and bottom. "The Aristocrat of Motor Oil" is white. "Cavalier/Motor/Oil" is lavender outlined in orange. Can has no top. All side are alike. Display 7/Reverse 6½. **$300**

5-gal "French Auto Oil" Ca 1915–1925. 14½" h. 9⅜" w. Can shows two racing cars speeding along on a track. Can is yellow, green, and red. "Marshall Oil Co./Distributors, U.S.A." is written in a circle. "Always Good/Try It" is in black letters at top and bottom on a yellow background. Display 7/Reverse 6. **$450**

5-gal "Nourse/Oils." Ca 1915–1925. 14½" h. 9⅜" w. A Viking is symbol in green and brown. "Nourse/Oils" is in white on a black background. "Jack Nourse Oil Co., Kansas City, Mo." is at the bottom. Display 8/Reverse 7½. **$150**

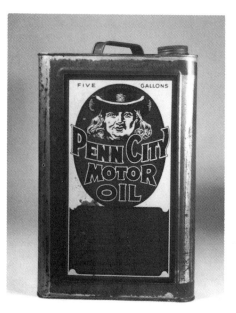

5-gal "Penn City/Motor/Oil." Ca 1915–1925. 14½" h. 9⅜" w. A quaker is symbol toward top in blue on red circle background. "Penn City/Motor/Oil" is blue with white outline. "Penn City National Oil Co./Philadelphia, PA" is written at the bottom. All sides are the same. Display 7/Reverse 6. **$75**

5-gal "Polarine" Motor Oil. Ca 1915–1925. 14½" h. 9⅜" w. Can pictures an early touring car on a yellow background. "Polarine" is blue outlined in light blue. "Standard Oil Company/ Indiana" is at the bottom. Picture is faded and has some paint loss. Display 6½/Reverse is in text. **$450**

5-gal "Polarine" Motor Oil. Ca 1915–1925. 14½" h. 9⅜" w. Can shows an early touring car in tropical weather and below zero weather. A thermometer divides these two scenes. Can is creme, car is black. "Standard Oil Company/An Indiana Corporation" is at the bottom. Display 7/ Reverse is text. **$475**

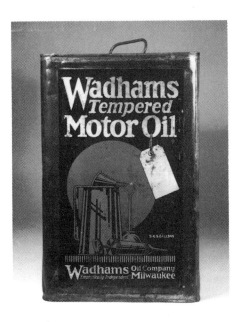

5-gal "Wadhams/Motor Oil." Ca 1915–1925. 14½" h. 9⅜" w. Black background. All lettering is white. Picture shows various oil containers in yellow and black. "Wadhams/Oil Company/Mil- waukee" is at the bottom. Display 6/Reverse 6. **$150**

Five-Gallon Easy-Pour Cans

5-gal Easy-Pour "Arrow/Motor Oil." Ca 1915–1925. 16¾" h. 14¼" dia. A black tin with "Arrow/Motor Oil" in a yellow circle. An arrow of red and yellow is in the center. "The Arrow Oil Co." is in yellow letters. Display 7/Reverse 6. **$250**

5-gal Easy-Pour "Autocrat/Motor Oil." Ca 1915–1925. 16¾" h. 14¼" dia. A yellow tin with "Autocrat" in red outlined in beige. A small circular picture of a polar bear is at the top. "Bayerson Oil Works/Erie, PA." is at the bottom. Display 7/Reverse 6. **$50**

5-gal Easy-Pour "Coreco/Motor Oil." Ca 1915–1925. 16¾" h. 14¼" dia. A golden yellow can with blue lettering outlined in white. "Continental Refining Co./Oil City, PA." is at the bottom. Display 7/Reverse 6. **$120**

5-gal Easy-Pour "Hyvis/Motor Oil." Ca 1915–1925. 16¾" h. 14¼" dia. A black tin with "Hyvis/Motor Oil" in white encircled in yellow. A red logo is in the center. "100% Pure" logo is at the top. Display 8/Reverse 7. **$110**

5-gal Easy-Pour "Kendall/Motor Oil." Ca 1915–1925. 16¾" h. 14¼" dia. A red can with a picture of a refinery "Kendall/Motor Oil" is white with black outline. Display 8/Reverse 7. **$110**

5-gal Easy-Pour "Keynoil." Ca 1925–1945. 14" h. 14¼" dia. White can with white eagle on red background standing on black mountain. Lettering is white outlined in red. "White Eagle/Oil and Refining Co./Kansas City, Mo." Original cap. Rust, scratches, and paint chipping. Display 7/Reverse 6. **$300**

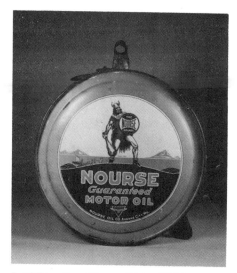

5-gal Easy-Pour "Nourse/Motor Oil." Ca 1915–1925. 16¾" h. 14¼" dia. A light blue can with a Viking on a hill and more Vikings in the background with a ship. "Nourse Oil Co., Kansas City, Mo." is at the bottom. Display 8/Reverse 7. **$300**

5-gal Easy-Pour "Penn/Empire/Motor Oil." Ca 1925–1945. 16¾" h. 14¼" dia. A blue can with a yellow circle with "Penn/Empire/Motor Oil" in white letters outlined in blue. "Empire/Oil Works, Inc./Oil City, PA." is at the top. Display 7/Reverse 6½. **$25**

5-gal Easy-Pour "Pennzoil/Safe Lubrication." Ca 1915–1925. 16¾" h. 14¼" dia. A yellow can with "Pennzoil" in black letters outlined in beige. A black and silver bell is behind. "The Pennzoil Company/Refinery/Oil City, Pennsylvania" is at the bottom. Display 7/Reverse 6. **$130**

CHAPTER 3

From Hood to Tailpipe:

Car Care Products in Individual Containers

Graphics, products, and company name can each be important to the collector of such items as antifreeze, car cleaner, and grease containers. The container may or may not still have some of the original product inside of it. Most items pictured here hail from before 1950.

Car Cleaners

"Fiebing's/Dressing." 16-oz. 4″ h. 3½″ w. Red with black car. White and black lettering. "Fiebing Chemical Co./Milwaukee, Wis." Very minor rust spotting. Dents on front of can and to sides. Display 7. **$20**

"Gulf/Gleam/Liquid/Gloss." 1-qt. 8″ h. 4¼″ w. Blue background with blue lettering. Orange and creme highlights. "Gulf Refining Co.—Pittsburgh, PA." Minor scratches. Display 8. **$50**

"Gree-Soff/Automobile Soap." Ca. 1930. 5¼″ h. 6¼″ dia. A dark blue can with an early automobile in yellow and blue on a gold background. All writing is in yellow. Compound is made with "Pure Linseed Oil." Has a handle. Scratches and small dents. Display 7. **$50**

"Klemco/Cleaner." Orange with brown lettering. Display 7. **$10**

"Mobilgloss/Cleans—Polishes—Protects Car Finishes." 6″ h. Very minor rust. Display 7. **$50**

"Simoniz" Can. Can is orange with red and black lettering. Display 8. **$15**

"Oilzum/Fabric/Cleaner" Can. 5 ¾″ h. 3″ w. Head of a man wearing glasses and a hat with the "Oilzum" logo in black at the top of the hat. Burnt orange original can color. "Manufactured By/ The White & Bagley Company/Worcester, Mass., U.S.A." at the bottom. Dents, minor rust, scratches, and wrinkles. Display 6. **$100**

"Stanocola/Liquid Gloss." 1-qt. 7½″ h. 4¼″ w. Yellow Can. "Stanocola" in black. "Liquid Gloss" in green on yellow rectangle outlined in black. "Standard Oil Company" emblem at bottom center. Soiled, scratches, and dents. Display 7. **$10**

67

Greases and Other Lubricants

"Atlantic Motor Grease." 5-lb. 5¼″ h. 6½″ dia. Red can with white lettering. "Atlantic" symbol in center of can. Dents, rust, and scratches. Display 6. **$15**

"Bellube Grease." 10-lb. 8″ h. 7½″ dia. Orange can with blue and white lettering. Has a handle. Blue bell trimmed in white with oil derrick in orange in center. "The Bell Oil and Gas Co." across the bottom. Scratches, dents, rust, and fading. Display 6½. **$10**

"Barnsdall/Lubricant." 5-lb. 7½″ h. 5½″ dia. Red can, blue and white lettering. "Barnsdall" across the top in blue outlined in white. Blue "B" in a blue and white square in the center. "Lubricant" near the bottom in blue outlined in white. "America's First Refiner" across bottom. Dents, rust, minor paint loss. Display 7½. **$20**

"Desmonds/Miracle/Oil." 32-oz. Overall soiling and minor rust. Display 7. **$15**

"Higrade/Cup/Grease." 10-lb. 7¼" h. 7½" dia. White can with red and black lettering. "Phillips/ Products" symbol top center. "Waite Phillips Company—Tulsa.Okla." across the bottom. Has a handle. Dents, rust, and fading. Display 6. **$45**

"En-Ar-Co/Lubricants." 5-lb. 7½" h. 5¾" dia. "En-Ar-Co/Lubricants" in red on yellow background. "Black Beauty/Axle Grease" in back. Boy holding chalkboard reading "National/Products Famous/Since 1882" on green background bottom center. Red stripe round bottom. Dents, rust, and soiling. Display 8. **$25**

"Finest Grease." 6" h. 6" dia. Blue pail on a yellow background. Lettering is blue. "Sun Oil Co. Philadelphia, Pa. U.S.A." Scratches and paint chipping overall. Dent to lid. Display 7. **$50**

"Mobilubricant." 16" h. 3⅝" dia. 3 lb. Vacuum Oil Company. Creme with black and creme lettering. Display 7. **$10**

Pep Boys "Pure As Gold" Grease Can. 5-lb. 5¼" h. Yellow can with Manny, Moe, and Jack at bottom. Yellow, black, and white lettering. Very minor scratches and soiling. Display 8½. **$25**

"P-H/Lubricant" Grease Can. 5-lb. 7½" h. 6" dia. Blue with golden yellow. Scenery of Bucktail Trail in Pennsylvania. Lettering is blue and black. Scene is blue, yellow, and white. "Industrial Oil Corporation/Warren, Pennsylvania, U.S.A." Very clean. Display 9. **$25**

"Pep Boys/Pure/As/Gold/Cup Grease." 1-lb. 3" h. 4¼" dia. White and black lettering. Yellow winged "Pure/As/Gold" with sunrays. Very Rare. Soiling and very minor scratches. One small dent. Display 7. **$150**

"Phillips/Grease." 5-lb. 7½" h. 5¾" dia. Yellow can. "Phillips Grease" in yellow on black circle in center of can. Other lettering in black at the top. "Bartlesville, Oklahoma" across bottom. Dents, scratches, and paint loss. Display 7. **$20**

"Supreme/Cup Grease." 25-lb. 10¾" h. 9¾" dia. Orange can with blue lettering. "Gulf Refining Co./Pittsburgh, PA." across the bottom. Pitting, rust, and dents. Display 6. **$10**

"Standard/Penetrating/Oil." 1-pint. Overall soiling and minor rust. Display 7. **$15**

"Texaco/Motor Cup Grease." 5-lb. Ca 1935–1945. 5¾" h. Can is green with Texaco symbol. "The Texas Company, Port Arthur, Texas, U.S.A." No handle. Scratches, rust, dents, and paint splotches. Display 7. **$50**

"Sunoco Greases." 5-lb. 5½" h. 6½" dia. Black with orange lettering and yellow highlights. Part full. Denting and soiling. Display 5. **$10**

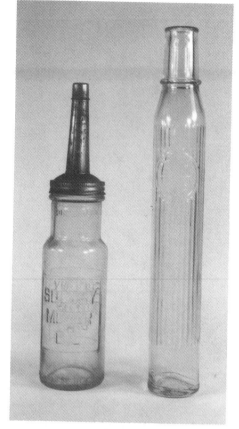

Left: "Tiolene" Glass Bottle. 1-qt. 18″ h. Embossed logo and lettering. Vertical embossed lines all the way around. Inside has very minor soiling. Display 8½. **$50**; *Right:* "Socony" Motor Oil Bottle. Glass. 1-qt. 15½″ h. Embossed lettering. Metal top with cap. Minor rust to metal lid and cap. Display 7. **$75**

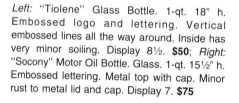

"Veedol Oils and Greases." 5-lb. Ca 1935–1945. 7⅞″ h. Can is red with creme circle. "Veedol/Oils and Greases" are black. A red "V" has creme wings with red and black bands. "Water Pump" is stamped at bottom. Fading, rust, and scratches. Display 7. **$10**

"Wearwell/Aviation Gun Grease." 5″ h. 5″ dia. Green Can. "Wearwell" in green against white across top. "Oil/Radio/Gas" in white in the center. "Aviation Gun Grease" in green on white near bottom. "Radio Oil Refineries Limited/Winnipeg, MAN." in white across the bottom. Minor flaking, dents, scratches, and rust. Display 8. **$25**

"White Eagle/Grease." 10-lb. 9″ h. 7¼″ dia. Red, black, and white can. White lettering outlined in black. Has a handle. "Socony-Vacuum Oil Company, Inc." in black on white. White eagle on sides. Scratches, rust, and dents. Display 7. **$35**

Antifreezes

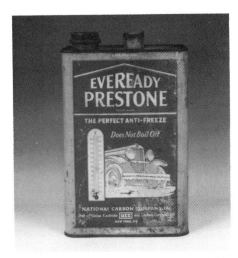

"Eveready/Prestone/Anti-Freeze." 1-gal. 9½″ h. 6½″ w. Orange, blue, and gray can outlined in orange. White letters. Picture of thermometer on left side with front end of an early auto with ice and snow hanging from the car. Handle and spout at the top. Minor rust and scratches. Display 8/Reverse 8. **$50**

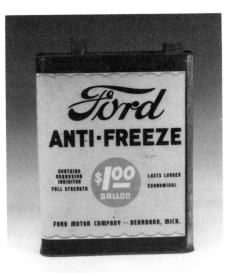

"Ford/Antifreeze." 1-gal. 10″ h. 8″ w. Yellow with blue border. Orange and black lettering. "Ford Motor Company—Dearborn, Mich." Minor rust at top and soiling. Display 7½. **$75**

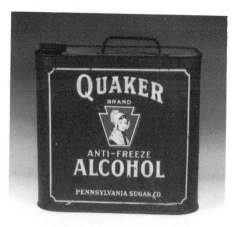

"Gulf/Cold Flo/Antifreeze." 1-qt. 5½″ h. 4″ dia. White background with red and blue lettering. Blue cars with blue snowflakes in background. "Gulf" logo at bottom center is blue and red. "Gulf Tire and Supply Company/Gulf Building, Pittsburgh, PA. U.S.A." Very minor rust and spotting. Display 7½. **$75**

"Quaker/Anti-Freeze/Alcohol." 2-gal. 8½″ h. 9½″ w. Deep blue can with white letters outlined in red. Picture of Quaker woman in the center. "Pennsylvania Sugar Co." across the bottom. Dents, rust, some fading, and paint splotches. Display 7½/Reverse 7. **$40**

"Zeroniz/Antifreeze." 1-gal. 5½″ h. 6½″ w. Blue with creme and red lettering. Eskimo with dogs and sled in front of igloos. "Manufactured by/ L.O. Church Corporation/Forrest, Illinois." Paint chipping and scratches. Display 6½–7. **$40**

Engine Products

"Fisk/Motor/Tune-Up." 16-oz. 5⅞" h. 3¾" w. "Fisk" in creme on burgundy across the top. "Motor/Tune-Up" in creme on burgundy across the bottom. "Fisk" tire logo in center in black and creme on creme background. Text on back. Scratches, small dent at bottom, and minor chipping to paint. Display 7½–8. **$40**

"Grate/Stuf!/Radiator/Seal." 5" h. Very minor scratching and denting. Display 7. **$10**

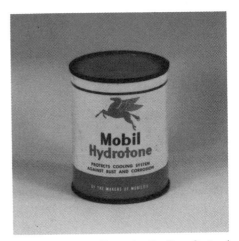

"Marvel Hi-Rev Motor Tune Up." 5" h. Minor scratching and soiling. Display 7½. **$10**

"Mobil Hydrotone/Protects Cooling System/ Against Rust and Corrosion." 3½" h. Very minor rust. Display 7. **$50**

"Whiz Commando/Rust Preventive." 5″ h. Very minor scratching and denting. Display 7. **$10**

"Nourse Power Plus." 5″ h. Minor scratching and soiling. Display 7½. **$10**

"Ward's/Vitalized/Engine Tone." 5″ h. Very minor scratching and denting. Display 7. **$10**

"Whiz/Kleen-Flush." 5½″ h. Very minor scratching and denting. Display 7. **$10**

CHAPTER 4

A Beacon Along the Way:

Signs for Every Purpose

Signs served as advertisements for the company owning the gas station, as well as for specific items available for sale in the station. Painted metal and tin signs were most common; but paper, porcelain, and cloth (for banners) were also used. Of course, good graphics and good condition are important in a collectible sign. Porcelain signs, which were common from about 1900 to about 1950, are among the most valuable and coveted signs.

Painted Metal Signs

"Cooper Tires" Sign. 12″ h. 48″ w. Blue with white lettering. Advertising both sides. Painted metal. Very minor scratching on both sides. Display 7½/Reverse 7. **$25**

"ALA" Sign. Ca 1941. 12″ h. 19¾″ w. Hanging painted metal. Oval. Dark blue background. Lettering is creme. Scratches, edgewear, fading, color stains on reverse, and dent. Display 7½/Reverse 6½–7. **$50**

"Armstrong/Rhino-Flex/Tires." 59″ h. 12″ w. Embossed painted tin. Yellow with black lettering. "G-91." Edges are dented overall. Very minor scratches. Display 7½. **$25**

"Pennzoil/Safe Lubrication" Sign. Ca 1958. 12″ h. 16½″ w. Die cut painted metal. Yellow with red bell in center and black lettering. Doublesided. Very minor scratching and rust spotting. Display 8/Reverse 8. **$50**

"Exide/You Start" Sign. 15″ h. 11¾″ w. Painted metal. Orange background with orange and black lettering. Picture of black and creme battery. Early black and creme car lower right corner. Edgewear, minor chipping. Display 8/Reverse 7. **$100**

"Wolf's Head" Curb Sign. 1953. 59″ h. Cast base with raised letters. Sign is green, white, and red with black and white lettering. Doublesided. Restored frame and stand. New paint. Looks great. Display 9+/Reverse 9+. **$250**

"Fire Chief Gasoline" Sign. 16″ h. 15½″ w. Painted metal. Red and white background. "FIRE CHIEF GASOLINE" in black across the top. Picture of red fire hat in top center. "Localized/For You" in white lettering. "In This Texaco Driving Area" in black. Scratches overall. Display 7. **$25**

Painted Tin Signs

"Atlantic/Paraffine Base/Motor Oil" Sign. 44" h. 14" w. Painted tin framed in wood. Blue and red lettering. "Aviation" overlaying blue plane. Logo has blue lettering with red crossed arrows and border. Denting and paint scratches. Chipping. Display 7. **$300**

"Battery Service/Our Batteries/Last Longer Cost Less" Sign. 9½" h. 27½" w. Painted tin with creme background and blue and black border. Lettering is embossed black. Blue "B" on white surrounded by a blue square on a raised rectangle outlined in black. Bent edges, scratches, rust. Display 7. **$40**

"Robert Bosch/Pyro Action/Spark Plugs" Sign. 12¼" h. 19⅜" w. Painted tin with yellow background with embossed red, yellow, and black lettering. Embossed spark plug to right side. Red embossed trademark lower right corner. Bent corners, wrinkled, and minor chipping. Display 7½. **$100**

"Cooper/Tires" Sign. 12" h. 32½" w. Embossed painted tin. Orange and blue background. Creme and blue lettering. Cooper tire to left side. "The Scioto Sign Co. Kenton, O," Scratches and minor denting to corners. Paint chipping. Display 7. **$100**

' "Firestone Tires" ' Sign. 11½" h. 35½" w. Embossed painted tin. "Firestone Tires" is orange lettered. "Most Miles Per Dollar" is creme. "Butternut Valley Hdwe. Co., Gilbertsville, N.Y." is in black lettering. Display 9. **$100**

"Goodrich/Safety Tread" Sign. 11½" h. 35¾" w. Embossed painted tin. Red and black with black and white lettering. Scratches and very minor fading. Corners dented. Display 8. **$300**

"B.F.Goodrich" Tire Sign. 23" h. 35" w. Painted tin. Blue with yellow and creme lettering. Tire in center. "Made in U.S.A. MCA-2-49 Property of the B.F.Goodrich Co. Akron, Ohio Stock No. 8-390-EG." at top edge. Very minor scratches. Display 8. **$20**

"Goodyear/Service Station" Sign. 12" h. 21¾" w. Flanged painted tin. Tire on left side. Lettering is orange, white, and black on a black and gray background. Goodyear logo in top center. Rust, scratches, and loss to luster one side. Display 7. **$50**

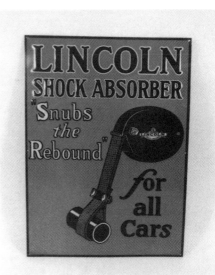

"Lincoln/Shock Absorber" Sign. 24" h. 17½" w. Painted metal tin. Ca 1915–1925. Orange sign bordered in black. "Lincoln/Shock Absorber" is black outlined in creme. "Snubs/the/Rebound" is creme outlined in black; "for/all/cars" is black. Sign pictures a black and creme "Lincoln/Shock Absorber." Scratches, bent, and paint loss. Display 7. **$75**

"Lodge/Spark Plugs" Sign. 12" h. 18" w. Painted tin. Yellow and black lettering. Picture of spark plug left side. "Lodge/Made in England" on white and pink accented in black. Scratches, bent edge, paint drips across top, paint chipped. Display 7. **$60**

"Premo/Auto Oil" Sign. 11" h. 36" w. Embossed painted tin. Die cut as an arrow. Red and creme background. Red, creme, and black lettering. "Independent Oil" in four corners. Very minor scratches and chipping to paint on corner tips and edges. Display 7½. **$100**

"Mobil/Tires" tin Sign. 48" h. 24" w. Embossed painted tin. Creme with blue lettering and border. Red Pegasus horse outlined in blue. Rare with "TIRES." Overall minor scratches and denting. Display 7. **$200**

"Marathon/Motor Oils" Sign. 13¾" h. 42" w. Tin framed sign. Contemporary green frame. Marathon runner standing beside early car on left side. Car is orange and creme. Lettering is creme and orange. Green background bordered in orange. Wrinkles, scratches, wear to paint on "M" in "Marathon" and beside "M." Display 8. **$900**

"Quaker State/Medium" Sign. 13½" h. 18½" w. Painted tin. Green with black border. Black and creme lettering. "Automobile Oil" in black at bottom. Quaker State logo in center in creme, green, and black. Very early Quaker State sign. Doublesided. Denting and minor scratches. Very minor rust. Display 7½/Reverse 7½. **$100**

"Magic/Gasoline" Sign. 24" h. 17¾" w. Painted Tin. Creme background. "Magic/Gasoline" black raised letters inside red gas globe. Red lightning bolts. Black highlights on globe. "Use" is black. Bent edges, scratches, edges are touched up. Some paint chips and wrinkles. Display 7. **$250**

Flanged Signs

"Auto-Lite/Service" Flanged Sign. 12½" h. 19" w. Painted metal. "Authorized/Service" in red on yellow background. "Auto-Lite" yellow on black background through center of sign. Creme background. Doublesided. Rust, scratches, and paint chipping. Display 7/Reverse 5. **$25**

"Firestone/Cycle Tires" Flanged Sign. 11½" h. 22" w. Painted metal. Red and white lettering. Navy blue background. Scratches and paint chipping overall, denting. Nail hole above "Tires." Display 6½. **$250**

"AC/Service" Flanged Sign. Ca 1947–1948. 18″ h. 10½″ w. Painted metal. "AC in orange on blue. "Service" is black on creme. Oil filter in yellow lettering on black hangs by S hooks. "Fuel Pump" in orange on black hangs by S hooks. Doublesided. Scratches, bent edge, rust, edgewear, minor splotches of paint on reverse side. Display 7½/Reverse 7. **$100**

Gulf "Supreme Auto Oil" Flanged Sign. Ca 1920. 18″ h. 2¼″ w. Porcelain. White background. Orange circle. "Supreme/Auto Oil" in dark blue letters shadowed in white and light blue. "LEAVES LESS CARBON" in dark blue. "Gulf Refining Company" in dark blue across the bottom. Wear to edge, rust, chipping to porcelain on "O" in "Oil" on reverse. "A" in "CARBON" on display side has chipping. Scratches and pitting. Display 6/Reverse 6. **$150**

Monogram "Greases/Oils" Flanged Sign. 15″ h. 24″ w. Porcelain. Red and white with red, black, and white lettering. Doublesided. Chipping to mounting holes on flange. Display 8½. **$300**

"Goodrich/Silvertowns" Flanged Sign. 19″ h. 23″ w. Porcelain. Deep blue background. "Goodrich/Silvertowns" is in debossed white letters. Two red debossed diamonds at the bottom. White line around oval shape. Doublesided. Loss to luster, edgewear, scratches, soiled, faded, and chipping to porcelain. Display 7/Reverse 6. **$200**

"Mopar/Parts" Flanged Sign. 16¾" h. 23¾" w. Painted metal. "MOPAR/PARTS" red lettering shadowed in blue on yellow oval surrounded by blue oval outlined in yellow. "Chrysler Corporation Engineered" in blue lettering. Other lettering in yellow. Doublesided. Scratches overall and edgewear. Display 6–7. **$100**

"Solite/Gasoline" Flanged Sign. 14" h. 18" w. Painted tin. White with red and white lettering. Blue triangle and two blue rings. Doublesided. Minor paint loss and rust. Display 6/Reverse 5. **$50**

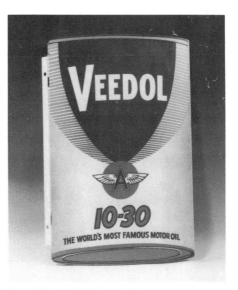

"Shell Gasoline" Flanged Sign. 17½" h. 22" w. Painted metal. Orange with red lettering and highlights. Doublesided. Scratches, paint chipping overall. Display 8/Reverse 8. **$350**

Veedol Motor Oil Flanged Sign. 18½" h. 24" w. Die cut tin. Blue flying A. Creme, blue, and gold lettering. Overall scratches. Display 7½–8/Reverse 7½–8. **$100**

Banners

"Put a Tiger in Your Tank" banner. Plastic. Yellow, orange, black, and white tiger covers the banner. Lettering is white on black. Soiled, left edge torn, creased. Display 8. **$100**

"Golden/Esso Extra" Banner. 83" h. 36" w. Canvas. Blue and white lettering. Gold and white pump with fluorescent orange at bottom. Crease across center and very minor soiling. Scratches to paint overall. Display 7. **$20**

"Veedol" Banner. 36" h. 58" w. Cloth. Red and black letters left side of banner. Blue and orange striped men's underwear hanging on clothesline. Robin on line above underwear. Soiled and water stained. Display 6. **$100**

"Giant Power" Banner. 34¼" h. 79" w. Cloth. Flying A top left corner. Black and red lettering. Giant is guiding car out of gas station. Gas station is "Tydol A/Veedol Motor Oils." Soiled and spotted. Display 7. **$50**

Socony Banner. 34" h. 99" w. Cloth. Red background with red and white lettering. Minor soiling. Display 8. **$40**

Paper Signs

"America's/lowest price/pickup truck." 24" h. 54" w. Yellow with red oval. White lettering. Small print in red lettering. Crease marks. Hole by "ow" in "lowest" and "e" in "priced." Display 7. **$25**

"Chalmers-Motor-Car-Co." 21" h. 20½" w. Blue lettering on creme. Center is blue with creme letters. "Guy Brewster Cady & Staff Inc./Detroit Agents For/Pal Brothers-Chicago" Shrink wrapped. Scratches overall. Tear to edge at left top. Three water marks along left side. Display 7. **$100**

Cambridge Cars Display Sign. 11" h. 20" w. Plastic coated. "The Cambridge Suburban 1928–1953" blue in color. Edges have very minor cracks and chipping. Display 8. **$25**

"Falcon" Poster. Yellow with red lettering. Has minor soiling and crease marks. Display 7. **$25**

"Wilson Needs/Henry Ford" Paper Sign. 12″ h. 37½″ w. Blue with white lettering. "Aston Print Det." Tears to edges. Very minor soiling. Display 7. **$50**

Cardboard Signs

Chevrolet Truck Cardboard Display Sign. 42″ h. 63″ w. Wood frame. Background is creme with various colored Chevrolet trucks. Lettering is black, orange, and yellow. Red eagle at top. Chevrolet logo bottom center. Great colors. Soiling and water mark along right side. Chips to wood frame. Display 7. **$200**

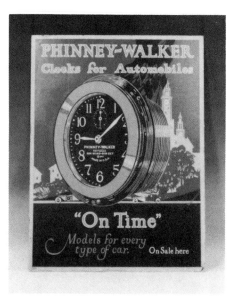

Neograph "Phinney-Walker" Cardboard Stand-up Sign. 20″ h. 15″ w. Orange and white lettering. Scene in background is yellow, blue, green, and orange. Label on back says "This is a Neograph Sign a new process patented in January 1918." "Schaefer-Ross Company, Inc./ Rochester New York" Minor tears to edges and nicks. Scratches under "Clocks." Display 7½. **$300**

Porcelain Signs

"American/Amoco/Gas" Sign. 15″ h. 24″ w. Porcelain. White background with white and black lettering on red background. Stars are red. Edgewear and minor rust, chipping around edges. Display 7½/Reverse 7. **$40**

"Automotive Maintenance/Association Inc." Sign. 18″ h. 20″ w. Hanging porcelain. "Independent/Member" yellow on deep blue. "Automotive Maintenance/Sacramento California/ Association Inc." is in blue lettering on yellow background. Stylized early car with "A.M.A. of S." outlined in blue on yellow. Emblem at bottom center blue and yellow. All letters are raised. Touch up to upper left. Overall displays fine. Display 7½–8. **$200**

"AMHA" 1951 Sign. 25″ h. 20″ w. Porcelain. "AMHA" in deep blue on yellow sunburst over orange circle. "American Motor Hotel Association" in white on deep blue. "Member/1951" is in white. Double-sided. Minor edgewear, very nice. Display 9. **$100**

"Carter/Carbureter/Service" Sign. 14½″ h. 32″ w. Porcelain. White background. "CARTER/ SERVICE" black letters trimmed in white on red background. "CARBURETER" in black lettering on white. Black border. Doublesided. Chipping to porcelain above "R" and "C" on display and edges. Scratches. Display 7½/Reverse 7. **$70**

"Curb-Service" Sign. 6" h. 24" w. Porcelain. Green background with white lettering and border. Edgewear, scratches, pitting along edges and chipping. Display 8. **$100**

"Gold Star" Sign. 30" dia. Porcelain. White with blue lettering. "100% Pure" logo to each side of yellow star with white oil derrick. "Star Oil Co." is in white lettering. Doublesided. Overall chipping on both sides. Display 6/Reverse 6. **$300**

"Mobiloil/Marine" Curb Sign Top. 31" dia. Porcelain. Blue and red lettering with red horse at top on white background. Chipping to porcelain under "Marine" on both sides. One chip goes all the way through. Display 8/Reverse 8. **$500**

"Magnolia/Gasoline" Round Sign. 42" dia. Porcelain. White lettering. Green and white flower. Advertising both sides. Overall chipping, rust, and cracking to both sides. Display 6/Reverse 5½. **$200**

"National/Automobile Club" Sign. 27" h. 30" w. Porcelain. Blue with blue and red lettering. White and blue eagle and map of United States. Doublesided. Chipping to mounting holes at edges. Display 8½/Reverse 8½. **$200**

"No Autos Filled/While Engines Running" Sign. 12″ h. 18″ w. Porcelain. Red background with white lettering. "Oil or Gas Lights Burning/Or Occupants Smoking." Edge bent lower right. Very nice. Minor chip to porcelain. Display 8½. **$200**

"76 Union" Round Sign. 22″ dia. Porcelain. Orange and white background. Lettering is orange and blue. Very clean. Display 9+. **$150**

"Power-lube/Motor/Oil" Sign. 20″ h. 28″ w. Porcelain. Doublesided. Yellow, black, and blue lettering. Royal blue background with white border. Orange tiger. Stamped "Wolverine Porcelain Detroit/This is Property of The Powerine Co." at bottom both sides. Minor scratching overall. Chipping to edges. Minor discoloration to porcelain. Display 8/Reverse 8. **$500**

"Sinclair Opaline/Motor Oil" Sign. 20″ h. 47¾″ w. Porcelain. Green sign with red border. Graphic of an oil can. Can is green and white striped on right side. Edgewear, chipping around edges, minor chip on white near right edge. Display 7½. **$500**

"Service" Sign. 59¼″ h. 9½″ w. Porcelain. Rocket shaped. Deep blue and white. White letters. Doublesided. Edgewear, chipping to porcelain around edges, paint speckles. Overall very nice display. Display 7½. **$200**

"Sterling/Motor Oil" Sign. 15″ h. 30″ w. Porcelain. "Sterling Oils" and "100% Pure" logos is yellow, red, and white. "Sterling" is white outlined in black on red. Rest is black lettering. Overall flaking and rust. Metal is chipped at edges. Display 6. **$100**

"Texaco/Crankcase/Service" Sign. 22″ h. 28″ w. Porcelain. Black, red, and yellow lettering on a white background. Texaco symbol top center. Black checkered border. Chipping to mounting holes and outer edges. Crack over "E" in "Texaco" and "C" in "Clean." Display 8. **$600**

"Willys/Jeep" Sign. 27″ h. 25″ w. Porcelain. "WILLYS" in creme on red. "Sales 'Jeep' Service" creme on deep blue. "E & S Motors/Sales & Service, Inc./Fitchburg" in black on creme. Doublesided. Minor edgewear, scratches, reverse side has paint chip on "O" on "Motor." Display 9/Reverse 8½. **$80**

"Zerolene" Sign. 27″ h. 27″ w. Porcelain. White with blue lettering. Blue and white logo at bottom. Overall chipping and cracking to porcelain. Display 7/Reverse 6. **$100**

CHAPTER 5

May I Help You?

Sales and Service-Related Items

This chapter includes everything from the patches and hats worn by gas station attendants to the display racks for various auto products, including maps and spark plugs. The advertising thermometers and clocks that adorned the station are also covered. Collectors looking to reconstruct an entire gas station will find much valued treasure here.

Clocks

"Amalie/Motor Oil" Clock. 15" dia. Glass front. Four Amalie cans at 12, 3, 6, and 9. Lettering is black and white. Very minor wear. Display 8 +. **$200**

"Michelin/X" Wall Clock. 14" h. 16" w. White plastic over metal back. "Michelin X" in yellow under white Michelin Man over a deep blue background. Numbers are white. Red metal minute hand. Clear plastic hour hands with white at the ends. Minor surface scratches, some chipping on metal. Display 8. **$100**

"Firestone" Clock. 15¼" h. 15¼" w. Square. Wood frame, glass front. Electric. Dark blue background on face. White numbers. "Fire-stone/Tires/Batteries/Spark Plugs/Brake Lining/and/Accessories" are in orange lettering. White hour hands and red second hand. Cord missing, torn at top left. Paint wear over word "Fire-stone." Frame chipped. Display 5–6. **$75**

"Oilzum/Motor Oil" Clock. 16" h. 16" w. Plastic. Creme with blue border. Creme and blue letter-ing. Oilzum man in orange and blue. Orange triangle in center. Numbering is creme. Metal back. Display 9. **$75**

"Oilzum/Motor Oil" Clock. 14½" dia. Glass face. Blue border with white center. Blue and white lettering. Oilzum Man in orange highlighted in blue. Lights up. Display 9. **$100**

"Studebaker" Clock. 15¼" h. 15¼" w. Dial electric. Gold metal rim. White background. "Studebaker" emblem top center in red and blue. "Studebaker" is blue letters. "Batteries" is in red. Black hour hands and markings. Red minute hand. Face cracked, scratches on rim. Small spots on glass. Rim slightly bent. Display 7. **$75**

"OK Quality Used Cars and Trucks" Clock. 15" h. 13" w. Plastic. Brown with yellow lettering and highlights. Hand is slightly bent. Display 8. **$20**

"Vanderbilt/Premium Tires" Clock. Ca 1958. 14½" dia. Glass face. Leopard in center jumping through red "V" with tire treads. Red, black, and white lettering. "Pam Clock Co. Inc. New Rochelle N.Y. circa '58." Very minor rust spotting. Display 8. **$100**

Thermometers

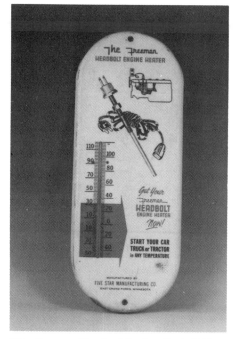

"Champion/Spark Plugs" Thermometer. 13½" h. 6½" w. Yellow with black and white spark plug in center. Reads "The Kemper Thomas Co./ Cinti., O. Made in U.S.A." at bottom of can on back. Very minor paint chips and soiling. Minor fading to paint. Display 7½–8. **$500**

"The Freeman/Headbolt Engine Heater" Thermometer. 15" h. 6" w. Painted metal. White with black and brown lettering. Picture of black and brown heater above thermometer. "Manufactured by/Five Star Manufacturing Co./East Grand Forks, Minnesota." Scratches and loss of luster. Display 7. **$50**

"Germania Refining Company" Thermometer. 9" dia. Glass front. Black lettering and numbers on white background. This company became Pennzoil. Scratches. Display 8. **$75**

"Gold Medal Motor Oils" Thermometer. 9⅛" dia. Painted metal. Round with glass. White background. Lettering is black. "Gold Medal Auto Oil" emblem is green, white, and black in the center. "The Kunz Oil Co./Since 1888." Wear to paint, rust, and pitting. Display 7½. **$150**

"Hood/Tires" Thermometer. 15" h. 4" w. Wood. White with man dressed in red and white. Lettering and numbers are white and black. "Dorfman Bros./Manufacturers of Advertising Thermometers/85–87 49th Street/Corona, N.Y." appears in small letters. Minor soiling. Display 7½. **$200**

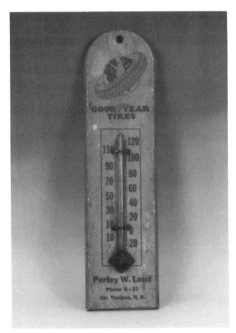

"Goodyear Tires" Thermometer. 11½" h. 3¼" w. Wood. Yellow with blue lettering and highlights. Goodyear Tire surrounding the globe. Soiling and very minor paint chipping. Display 7. **$50**

"Pennzoil" Thermometer. 12" dia. Orange and black lettering and numbering. Orange Liberty Bell. Very minor mildew at bottom. Display 7. **$150**

"Oilzum" Thermometer. 15″ h. 7½″ w. Painted tin. Black lettering with head of a man on left side of thermometer. Burnt orange background. "Oilzum" on his hat. "The White & Bagley Company/Worcester, Massachusetts, U.S.A." "The Choice of Champion Race Drivers." Thermometer is white with burnt orange markings. Minor scratches and flaking, small dent on left edge. Display 8. **$350**

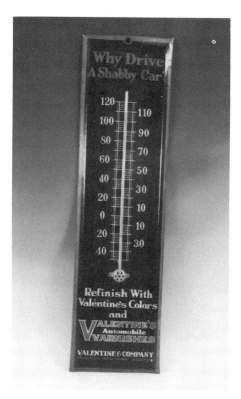

"Valentine's Automobile Varnishes" Thermometer. 20″ h. 5½″ w. Celluloid. Black with red border. Red and creme lettering. "Valentine & Company/Chicago New York Boston" Dent at top and very minor soiling. Display 8. **$100**

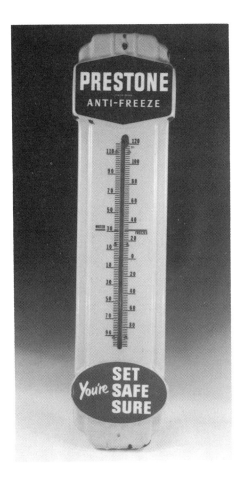

"Prestone/Anti-Freeze" Advertising Thermometer. Ca 1940s. 36″ h. 8¾″ w. Porcelain over metal. Background is gray with blue "Prestone" logo at top. "You're Safe And You Know It" in white over red at bottom. Chipping to porcelain around edges and scratches. Display 7½–8. **$75**

Product Displays and Salesman's Samples

"Astrostar Tires" Rack. 9″ h. 13″ w. Painted tin. Black and brilliant green. Aircraft in center top. Very minor scratches. Display 8. **$45**

"Auto Lite Spark Plugs" Cabinet. 18½" h. 13 ⅛" w. Painted metal. Green cabinet. Glass front. "Auto Lite/Spark Plugs/Ignition Engineered By Ignition Engineers" in yellow on blue background at the top on die cut metal. Tin-stacked Auto Lite Spark Plug boxes are seen through the clear glass on each side. Back is hinged to open and reveal storage area. Rust, scratches, fading, and dent. Display 7–7½. **$45**

"Boyce/Moto Meter" tin Sign. 19" h. 12" w. Embossed. Die cut. Shades of green. Shape of moto meter. Red, black, and creme lettering. "The Motometer Co. Inc./Long Island City, N.Y. U.S.A." Stands up. Rare item. Minor rust below and above company name and around edge on right side. Display 7½. **$700**

"Buss Auto Fuses" Display. 7½" h. 8½" w. Yellow and creme lettering. Man scratching head alongside road with his car as other cars are passing. Display has 10 fuse boxes. Minor soiling and denting at top. Display 7–7½. **$50**

"Blue Crown" Spark Plug Display in original box. 16½" h. 14" w. Tin. Blue with blue, black, gray, and white sparkplug. White and blue lettering. Very clean. Display 9 +. **$150**

"Champion/Spark Plugs" Display. 12" h. 18" w. 5½" deep. Tin. Yellow with black lettering. "Champion" is white embossed. Spark plugs on front. Minor rust, denting, and soiling. Display 7. **$150**

"Cornell/Tube/Repair Kit." Ca 1933. 8½" h. 3½" dia. Yellow and creme lettering. Black, yellow, green, and creme background. "Ca. 1933 By Cornell Tire and Rubber Co." Minor rust and scratches. Display 7. **$50**

"Edison Mazda" POP Light. 24¼" h. 14½" w. Painted tin. Deep blue box. Hinged door opens to reveal gray shelves and gray light bulb holders containing two automobile lamps. Picture of woman in early dress holding box of automobile lamps on the side. "Edison/Mazda/Automobile/ Lamps" on front and back in orange. GE logo and Edison Mazda logo on front and back. Scratches, edgewear, and paint wear. Very nice piece. Display 8. **$250**

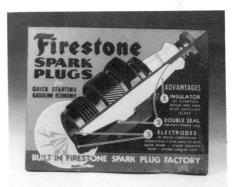

"Firestone/Spark/Plugs" Display Cabinet. Ca 1940–1950. 15¼" h. 20⅛" w. Painted tin. Shows colorful detailed graphic of spark plug. Spark plug is black and white with gray highlights. "Firestone/Spark/Plugs" in blue lettering outlined in black over orange. Bottom of sign is green with green and white lettering. Very minor scratches and rust. Display 8. **$250**

"FORD" POP Light Bulb. Ca 1960s. 26″ h. 11″ w. Plastic. Light bulb on black base. "Ford" logo on top. "See the Light!" on top of the base. Very nice piece, hard to find. Display 9. **$100**

"Gulf" Rack. 25½″ h. Metal with tin sign. Beige with orange and blue logo. Doublesided. Rust spotting overall. Display 5/Reverse 5. **$60**

"Ford" Motor Oil Display. Metal. 25″ h. 18″ w. "The Motor Oil/from the/Motor Company." Blue and white lettering on a white background. Scratches overall. Display 7. **$65**

"Gilmer/SuperService/Moulded Rubber/Fan Belt" Counter Display. 22¼" h. 16½" w. 24" d. Painted tin. Orange box with blue trim. Advertising on four sides. Color picture of man smoking cigar on the front. He is holding a "Gilmer" fan belt. Lettering is dark blue, creme, and black. Five display shelves are black tin. Scratches, top has wrinkles, some paint loss. Still able to display nicely. Display 8. **$250**

"Hood Tube" Box. 13" h. 5" w. 5" deep. Cardboard. Hood Tire Man in red and creme. Lettering is creme. Directions on top of box. Creasing and soiling. Tears. Rare. Display 6½. **$150**

"Hastings/Oil Filters" Display. 16" h. Creme, yellow, pink, black, and orange. Creme, orange, and black lettering. Hastings oil filter included. Fading at bottom. Soiling. Display 7½. **$50**

Mayo-Skinner Die Cut Cardboard Wiper Display. 27½" h. 31¾" w. Man in blue suit with gray stripes and white and gray checkered hat sitting inside car looking out clear windshield into pouring rain. Train and railroad crossing is seen through windshield. Red and white lettering. Wear to edges. Everything connected. Display 8. **$500**

103

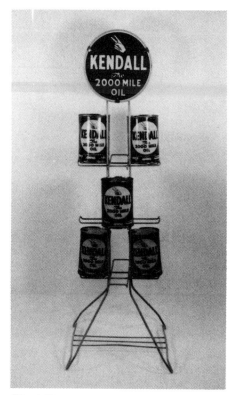

"Micro-Lube" Lubrication Display. 34" h. 20" w. Metal. Red and blue background. White and yellow lettering. Plane is red, yellow, and blue. Yellow and red background. Very minor scratches. Display 8. **$75**

"Kendall/2000 Mile" Display Rack and Cans with original box. Rack 39½" h. 13" w. 13" deep. 1-qt. cans are red with black band at bottom. White car, truck, boat, and bus. Red lettering. Rack is gray with red sign at top. White lettering. Box has red and black lettering. Box has oil staining. Cans and rack have minor scratches and rust spotting. Rack: Display 7. Cans: Display 7. **$300**

"Mirro/Like" Auto Products Display. 19½" h. 13" w. 10¼" deep. tin. Blue with yellow, creme, and blue lettering. Overall soiling and scratches. Display 7. **$50**

8-qt. 'Mobiloil "AF" ' Rack. 22″ h. Metal wire. Red with white lettering outlined in black. Restored all sides. Caps are new. Display 8. **$500**

"Niehoff" Light-Up Sign. 11¼″ dia. Metal rim, glass face. Rim is gold. "Authorized Distributor" is creme. "Niehoff" lettering is red shadowed in black on creme background. "Automotive Products" is in black lettering. Red circle surrounded by blue markings. Back is loose, rust, scratches, and scuff marks. Display 6½–7. **$30**

"Mohawk" Tires Rack. 8″ h. 15″ w. Painted tin. Green and yellow lettering on white. Mohawk logo in corner. Advertising on both sides. Very minor scratches and soiling. Display 8–8½. **$60**

"Schrader/Tire Gauge." Ca 1920–1930. 14¾″ h. 6″ dia. Red can with a black top. "Test Your Tires/Every Friday/It's A Saving/Habit" is in blue letters. Picture of gauge is silver and black. Hinged door opens for storage of gauges. Rust and wear to paint. Display 7. **$160**

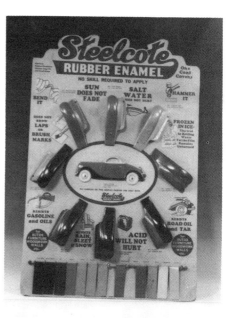

"Shell" Oil Bottle Storage Case. 15" h. 14¾" w. 11⅝" deep. Metal with hinged lid. Early case. "SHELL" stamped on lid has slots for 16 glass bottles of which 10 are filled with Shell bottles. Bottles are clear glass and 14½" h. All have logo on them. Case is newly painted black. One bottle has minor rim damage. Others are fine. Display 8. **$250**

"Steelcote Rubber Enamel" POP Display. 29¾" h. 19¾" w. Cardboard display. Metal color chart across the bottom. Early car in center surrounded by two-tone fenders all are metal in various colors. Lettering is blue. Various advertising promises on display. Minor paint wear, edgewear, creases. Rare item. Display 8½. **$500**

"Steel Super-X Oil Ring" Paper Mache Bone. 24" l. Black and red lettering. White bone. Chipping overall. Very rare. Display 6½–7. **$50**

"Sunoco" 8-Bottle Rack. 14½" h. Metal wire. Four have blue lids and caps. Four have silver with blue caps. New plastic caps. All have blue and yellow "Sunoco" label. Not a matched set. Some labels are faded or chipping off. Rack has minor chipping. Display 7½. **$400**

"X-Power" POP Counter Stand. 15" h. 11" w. Cardboard display. Orange. ' "X" Power/Repairs/Leaky Radiators' Young boy in black pouring "X" Power in early car. "Price 35 cents." Folds out to A frame to stand up. Minor tears and creases. Dents to cardboard cans. Display 6½–7. **$100**

"Whiz/Patch Outfit" Display. 21¼" h. 14½" w. Painted metal. Blue with white and yellow letters. Orange, green, and yellow graphic. Very minor fading and paint chipping. Very scarce. Display 8. **$300**

Hats

"Casper Brake & Clutch Co." Lubrication Hat. Very minor wear. Display 8. **$10**

"Grey Rock" Lubrication Hat. Very minor wear. Display 8. **$10**

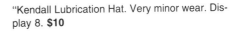

"Kendall Lubrication Hat. Very minor wear. Display 8. **$10**

"RPM/Motor Oil/Lubricants" Hat. Very minor wear. Display 8. **$10**

"Mobil" Hat with correct buttons. All original. Brown in color with Mobil patch of creme bordered in blue. Red horse and blue lettering. Rim at very front is cracked. Patch has minor soiling. Display 8½–9. **$150**

Arm Patches

"Getty" Arm Patch. 2⅞" h. 4½" w. Soiling. Display 7½. **$5**

"American" Arm Patch. 2⅜" h. 3" w. Minor soiling. Display 8. **$5**

"Chevron Supreme Gasoline" Arm Patch. 2¾" dia. Minor soiling. Display 7½. **$5**

"Citgo" Arm Patch. 2 ⅜″ square. Minor soiling. Display 7½. **$5**

"Shell" Arm Patch. 2″ square. Minor soiling. Display 7½. **$5**

"Gulf" Arm Patch. 2¼″ h. 2½″ w. Minor soiling. Display 8. **$5**

"Sunoco" Arm Patch. 2″ h. 2¾″ w. Minor soiling. Display 8. **$5**

"Mobil" Arm Patch. 1¼″ h. 3⅛″ w. Minor soiling. Display 8. **$5**

"Texaco" Arm Patch. 2″ h. 3¼″ w. Minor soiling. Display 7½. **$5**

Maps and Map Holders

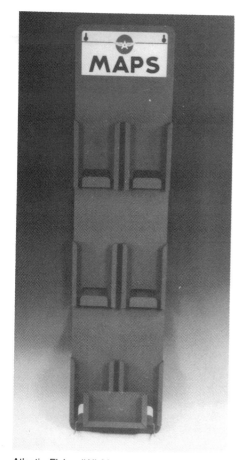

"Calso/Gasoline" Map Holder. 20″ h. 12½″ w. Three shelves. Red painted metal. "Road" in white letters at top left. "Maps" in white letters at top right. "Calso/Gasoline" in top center surrounded by a white circle. Rust, paint chips, scratches, small dent top left. Dents on back, wear on paint. Display 7. **$75**

Atlantic Flying "A" Map Holder. 36″ h. 8½″ w. Red with black lettering. Flying A in center. Display 9. **$80**

Map Rack. 16¼″ h. 14″ w. Painted white metal. "It's So Easy/To Say . . . /Charge It." Soiling and minor scratching. Display 7½. **$10**

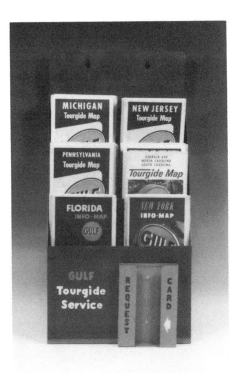

"Gulf/Tourgide/Service" Map Holder. 18″ h. 9⅛″ w. Three racks. Blue metal. Lower left "Gulf" in orange. "Tourgide" in white. "Service" in white lower right has an orange holder for request cards. Complete with Gulf maps from various states. Some duplicates. Very good condition, some paint scuffing on front and sides. Display 7. **$50**

Phillips 66 Maps. Maps are of various States. Display 7. **$90**

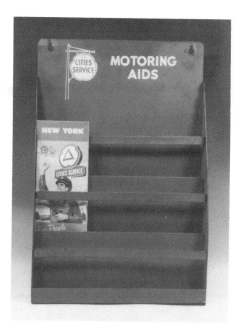

"Cities/Service" Map Holder. 19″ h. 13″ w. Three shelves. Green painted metal. Lettering is white. Rust, dent, and paint chipping. Display 7. **$75**

"Texaco/Touring/Service" Map Holder. 9″ h. 4″ w. 2½″ deep. Painted metal. Green with red shield. White lettering. Maps included. Very minor scratches. Display 8. **$75**

Miscellaneous

Early "Chevrolet" Hub Cap. 10″ dia. Painted metal. Gray with black lettering. Scratches and rust. Display 7. **$15**

Dietz Ideal Motor Headlamps, Pair. Ca 1897. 11½″ h. 6½″ w. Polished brass. "Pat'd Nov. 24-03". "Dietz N.Y. U.S.A." on the knobs that raise and lower the wick. Oil lamps, professionally polished. "Dietz" on nameplate on side of lamps. Minor scratches, dents on base and top. Slightly tarnished. Display 6. **$250**

"Motor-Tunometer." 13″ h. 13½″ w. Metal casing. Polarity switch, battery check selector, and calibrator knobs—one in each of four corners on silver background. Glass face and cord attached. "Echlin" emblem lower center of performance chart. Red, yellow, and blue colors on the chart. Black lettering. Paint loss, soiled, rust, and scratches. Display 7. **$25**

Tidewater Credit Card Machine. 6¼″ h. 14″ w. 11½″ deep. Metal. "Serial No. 067348" Red and silver. "Farrington Manufacturing Company Needham Heights, Mass." 'Flying "A" Credit Service' on side. "Patent No. 2620736/Patent No. 2606494" Crowther Filling Station Stamp and note pads included. Paint chipping and scratches. Display 7. **$75**

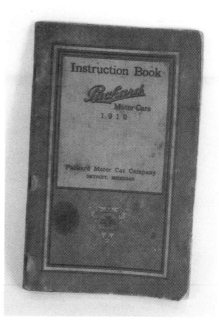

"Instruction Book/Packard/Motor Cars." Ca 1910. 8½″ h. 5½″ w. Paper. 56 pages. Lettering throughout the book is done in black and orange. Illustrations are black and white with orange lettering. Book is soiled and edges are worn, stained, spotted, and faded. Display 6– 6½. **$50**

CHAPTER 6

Take It Home:

Premiums, Giveaways, and Other Souvenirs

Even today, many gas stations offer souvenir glasses and toys to customers who get a "fill-up." Collectors who are focusing on items from a particular company will want to collect the toy models, salt shakers, and other figural items depicting the company's logo or representative characters. License plate attachments are a more rare souvenir of auto-related companies. These were attached to the car, and the license plate hung from their hook. They were in use from about 1900 to the 1940s.

Pins

"Flying A Quality" Pinback. 1″ dia. Red and creme with black and red lettering. Rust to back of pin. Display 8. **$5**

"Red Lion" Pinback. 1″ dia. Creme with red lion and red and black lettering. "Vichrome Inc. L.A. & S.F." on back. Minor scratching. Display 7. **$15**

"Koolmotor/Bronze Gasolene" Pinback. 3″ dia. Yellow and black with red, yellow, black, and white lettering. Rust to back of pin. Display 8. **$5**

Ashtrays and Lighters

"Conoco" Cigarette Lighter. 1¾" h. 2" w. Gold and silver with cowboy holding branding iron of Conoco logo. Lettering is orange and black. Conoco logo of orange and gold on back. Very minor wear. Display 8/Reverse 8. **$20**

Mack Ashtray. 4½" h. Silver. "Design/Patent/87931." Display 9. **$20**

"Michelin" Man Ashtray. 4½" h. 5½" dia. Ashtray is creme and brown base. Soiling. Display 7½. **$50**

License Plate Attachments

"Automobile Club of Pittsburgh" License Plate Attachment. 3½" h. 3½" dia. Porcelain. white background. Black lettering. Emblem is maroon and green with white lettering and black outline. Scratches, edgewear, rust, minor chipping. Display 7½. **$50**

"Illinois Farm Bureau" License Plate Attachment. 4½" h. 3¾" w. Porcelain. Yellow and black lettering on blue and red background. State of Illinois is red and yellow with black. Early car. Background of country scene in yellow and black. Very minor wear at bottom of "Bureaus" Display 8. **$80**

"D-X" License Plate Reflector. 4" h. 5½" w. Red with yellow lettering. "Dura-Products Mfg. Co./ Canton, Ohio/Patented." Very minor rust and scratches. Display 7½. **$10**

"Tydol" License Plate Attachment. 6¾" h. 3½" w. Painted tin. Tydol Man is yellow carrying lube can outlined in black. Black lettering raised. Slight scratching and paint wear. Display 8. **$75**

Calendars

"Magnolia" Mobiloil 1933 Calendar. 23″ h. 14″ w. Months of August, July, and September. Mobiloil logos at bottom and top. Car in mountain scene with plane flying over. Ship on water in center. Water mark across half of calendar. Tear to "N" in "Magnolia." Display 6. **$50**

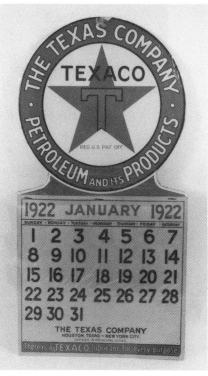

"Texaco" Die Cut Calendar. 25″ h. 13″ w. Calendar intact. Top is red, white, black and green. Calendar has red and black lettering and numbering. "The Texas Company/Houston, Texas—New York City." Paper has yellowed. Tear to top at "S" in "Texas" has been taped. Display 8. **$100**

"Chevrolet/Motor Cars" 1920 Calendar. 30½" h. 16" w. Green with white lettering. Calendar pages are gray with black lettering and numbering. Lithograph of country scene and family. Very minor creases and black metal at bottom missing on left side Also small tear from left side at bottom. Display 7. **$75**

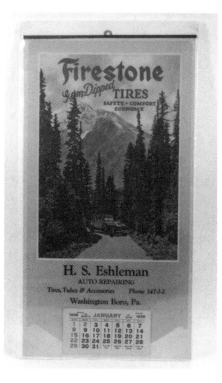

"Firestone" 1928 Calendar. Calendar intact. Black lettering. Early car on road with mountains in background. Greens, purple, blues, white, and red. Crease at top. Display 7. **$100**

"Socony/Gasoline & Motor Oil" Calendar. 26½"
h. 13½" w. Pictures service man holding hose to
red Socony gas pump. Early car in background.
Display 6. **$90**

Salt and Pepper Shakers

"Esso" Salt and Pepper Shakers. 2¾" h. 1" w.
¾" deep. Plastic. Pepper is red and white with
red and white logo decals. Salt is blue and white
with same color. Logo decal. "W.W. Kirkpatrick/
Ea./-3600." Decals are cracking. Display 8. **$20/
pair**

"Phillips 66" Salt and Pepper Shakers. 2¾" h. 1" w. 1" deep. Plastic. Orange with creme, black, and orange decals. "Slycard Garage Reasoner, Iowa Phone 44-14" on back. Bottom to "Ethyl" is melted and deformed. Minor soiling. Display 8. **$45/pair**

Banks

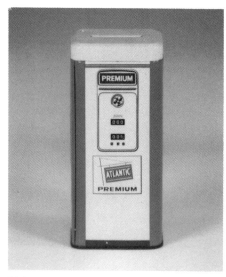

"Atlantic" Pump Bank. Tin. 5" h. Red and white. Tin with red, white, blue, and black lettering and highlights. Blue bottom. Lid on top is white. Display 9+. **$45**

"Esso" Bank. 6½" h. Plastic. Red man saluting. Red, white, and blue Esso logo on his chest. Six very minor melted spots at base and one on his right leg. Display 8. **$100**

Waxed Cardboard Banks. 5½" h. 4" dia. *Left:* "Drydene/Dieselall/Motor Oil"; *Center:* "Zephyr/Motor Oil"; *Right:* "Pennzoil . . . GT Performance." Display 9+. **$50 for all three**

"Esso" Glass Block Bank. 4¾" h. 4¾" w. Embossed "Esso." "Watch/Your Savings Grow/With/Esso." Display 8½–9. **$50**

Tin Banks. *Left:* "Sunoco" bank is yellow and blue. 3½" h. *Right:* "Conoco" bank is red, green, and white. 3¾" h. Very minor scratching. Display 8. **$35 for the two**

Toys

"Mobilgas" Tanker Truck Toy. 2½" h. 9" l. Tin. Red with black highlights. Cab door has "Ford" in blue, yellow, and creme. Mobilgas is creme outlined in black. Logo is in center of lettering. Rubber tires. Plastic clear hose. "Made in Japan B.C." Very minor overall scratches. Display 8. **$150**

Early Pumps Marx Toy. 6" h. Pair. 9½" w. Tin with milkglass globes. Battery operated. One pump is blue and yellow and the other is red and black with creme highlights. Center cabinet reads "Oil—Grease Anti-freeze Compounds." Marx logo on front of each pump. In/Out signs are orange and black. "American Made." Overall scratches and fading to paint. Display 7. **$250**

"Shell" Tootsietoy Tanker Truck. 1¾" h. 6" l. Pressed steel. Orange. "Shell" raised lettering with seashells on each side of lettering. Overall scratches and paint chipping. Display 7. **$50**

"Gas" Pump. 6½" h. Cast Iron. Red with rubber gas hose. Crank on back turns dial on front. Gold lettering and numbering. Overall paint loss. Display 7½. **$150**

"Sinclair" Tanker Truck Marx Toy. 18½" l. Green with black and white and red highlights. Lettering on tank car is creme, and green and red on truck cab. Marx logo is on bottom of cab door. Tin tires say "Louis Marx & Co. Inc. RM." Very minor scratches overall. Displays 8½–9. **$400**

"Texaco" Toy Tanker Boat with Box. 5" h. 26½" l. Plastic. Motorized. Texaco logo on stack. Burnt red and black ship. "Texaco North Dakota" in white. Depth markings are white. Wheels on the bottom. Very nice piece. Some paint scuffing. Display 9. **$150**

Miscellaneous

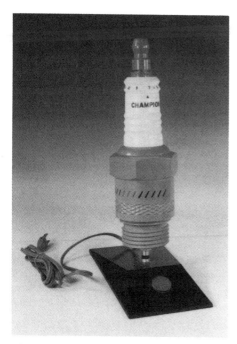

"Champion" Plug Radio. 14″ h. Gray and white spark plug. "Champion" red lettered. Gold label at center on base. "Champion/Dependable/ Spark Plugs" Display 8½–9. **$50**

"Coreco" Glass. 4¾″ h. Red and yellow lettering on yellow and black background in shape of Pennsylvania. "100% Pure" logo at bottom in black. Very minor wear to lettering. Display 8. **$25**

"Dodge/Job-Rated/Trucks" Miniature Clip-board. Ca 1940s. 5½″ h. 3″ w. Painted metal. Blue with yellow lettering and label with writing. Writing on label is rubbed off. Display 7. **$5**

"Chevrolet Dealer" Cigar Box. Ca 1937. 2½" h. 12" w. 9¼" deep. Syroco wood. "Chevrolet Dealer/Used Car Committee/1937" and the "Chevrolet" logo are embossed on the lid in the center of a diamond. Hinged lid. Wooden box inside. Fancy presentation box. "Syroco Wood/ Made In the U.S.A." sticker on the bottom. Aged look. Scarce Item. Very nice piece. Display 8. **$100**

"Fisk" Tire glasses, Six with Box. 4⅝" h. 2–2½" dia. Genuine Libby Safedge Tumblers. Guarantee on side of box. Picture of boy in sleeper holding a candle and leaning against a tire. "Time to Retire" at the bottom under picture. "Piedmont/Tire Service, Inc./121 South Main St./Winston-Salem, N.C./Phone 5-2421/Modern Recapping." Very good condition. Display 7. **$50 for six and box**

"Gulf Member 3% Club" Pocketknife. 3" l. Blue and orange lettering and Gulf logo. Advertisement on one side only. Display 8. **$40**

"Get a Fisk" Print. 1926. 14" h. 11" w. Wood framed print. White background picture of two boys in early attire, one walking on advertising sign. "Get a Fisk" in orange. "Time to Re-Tire" in light blue. Fisk logo on sign. Sign is wedged in small tree with beehive and bees flying from hive at lower right side of print. Wear to frame, print in good condition. Display 8. **$50**

Left: "Ray Cotton Company" Truck Inkwell. 3¾" h. 8" w. 3" deep. Cast iron top of truck bed lifts to expose inkwell. Embossed lettering. Driver inside. "Ray Cotton Company/Franklin Mass/ Agents Cotton Mills/Waste Association." Hooks on side to hold pen. Minor soiling. Display 7½. **$80**; *Right*: "Master Trucks" Inkwell. 5½" h. 7" w. 2¾" deep. Cast iron. Embossed lettering. Truck back is inkwell and stones lift to expose inkwell. Driver inside. "Master Trucks, Inc. Chicago, U.S.A." Very detailed. Hinge is broken on inkwell lid. Display 7½. **$80**

"Maxim Motor Company/75th/Anniversary" Presentation Pen and Pencil Set. 6" h. 11" w. 10" deep. Wood base with gold embossed graphics and lettering. Cast Iron. Maxim Motor Co. is a firetruck manufacturing company in Middleboro, Mass. Display 8. **$25**

"Phillips 66" Paperweight Mirror. 3½" dia. Black and silver with black and silver lettering. Phillips 66 logo is in center. Display 7. **$100**

Tiger Tails. Box of yellow and black tails with red streamers. Texaco the Tiger promotional giveaways. Display 9. **$30**

Miniature Gas and Tax Price Stand. 10½" h. 6½" w. Metal frame with cardboard center with black lettering. Several cards are with this sign. Doublesided. Minor soiling and paint loss to frame. Display 7. **$75**

Miniature "Texaco Fire Chief" Fireman's Hat. 8″ h. Red plastic hat with gold eagles head holding creme colored shield. "1" in gold on back. Texaco symbol center of shield. Red lettering. Very minor scratches. "1" is pulled up at edges. Display 8. **$50**

Blotters. Sizes range from 3½″ to 4″ h and 5½″ to 9″ w. *From left to right:* "Wolf's Head/Oil," "Sunoco/Oil," "Texaco/Motor Oil." Display 8½–9. **$100 for all three**

APPENDIX A
Abbreviations Used in This Book

/	indicates the beginning of a new line of writing
" "	indicates writing that appears on the item
ca	circa
dia	diameter
deep	deep
gal	gallon
h	high
l	long
lb	pound
NOS	new old stock
oz	ounce
POP	point of purchase
qt	quart
w	wide

APPENDIX B
A History of the Oil Industry

Oil! The very word conjures images of excitement, of industrial might, of undreamed riches. Oil powers our vehicles, lubricates our machines, and is the basis for many spinoff industries (like plastics). Oil is the fuel that made America (and indeed the entire world) what it is today. Without it, the economy of the world would collapse.

Few people realize, however, that initially oil was valued primarily for its medicinal qualities, and that during the first 40 years in the history of the oil industry, it was used primarily as an illuminant. Few others realize that without the automobile, the industry likely would not have become the giant that it is today.

The oil industry traces its roots to western Pennsylvania. It was there that Col. Edwin L. Drake drilled the first oil well, thereby setting into motion a chain of events that resulted in the creation of one of the mightiest industries the world has ever known. The story, however, goes back much further. Oil is mentioned in the Old Testament (Job), by Herodotus, and by other sources.

The Pennsylvania oil region had an apocryphal "history" of fire on water supposedly written by the French Commander of Fort Duquesne in a letter to His Excellency, General Montcalm. This particular letter turned out to be fiction. It was published in the early 1840s, but is repeated here because of the effect that it had. It said:

While descending the Allegheny, fifteen leagues below the mouth of the Conewango, and three above Venango, we were invited by the Chief of the Senecas to attend a religious ceremony of his tribe. Gigantic hills begirt us on every side. The Great Chief recited the conquest and heroism of their ancestors. The surface of the stream was covered with a thick scum, which burst into complete conflagration. The oil had been gathered and lighted by a torch. At the sight of the flames, the Indians gave forth a triumphant shout that made the hills echo and re-echo again. Here, then, is revived the ancient fire worship of the East. Here, then, are the Children of the Sun.

(F.W. Beers, 1865 Atlas of the Oil Region of Pennsylvania).

The region they described was probably the Oil Creek Valley in Venango County, Pennsylvania, about 100 miles north of Pittsburgh. It was on the banks of this creek that Col. Drake drilled three wells, the first in 1859. It was this event that signaled the birth of the oil industry.

Although the preceding description was fiction, use of petroleum by native Americans is well documented. The early Indians and perhaps visitors from afar left many enigmatic pits in the alluvium of valley bottom lands, especially along Oil Creek. Timothy Alden, the first president of Allegheny College, Meadville, Pennsylvania, described these pits in 1820. He said:

On the flats of Oil Creek, 28 miles southeasterly from Meadville, many oblong pits have been dug several feet deep, from the bottom of which the Seneca oil, or petroleum, oozes and floats on the surface of the water, with which they are partially filled. Some of these are of unknown antiquity; and whether the work of the French, who in the former part of the last century had military establishments on our principal streams, or of that people, of whom no tradition has reached our times, but whose judgment and skill in the art of fortifying there are numerous evidences, it is impossible to resolve.

By extending this operation, this oil, called by the Senecas 'au nus' might be collected so as to become a profitable article of commerce. Fifteen barrels were once taken in one season from a single pit. It was formerly sold at two dollars a gallon. The common price is now one dollar and fifty cents. It is one of the most penetrating liquids in nature. No wooden nor earthen vessel is impervious to it. Even glass, in which it is stored for some time, cannot be cleared of its scent. This oil is much esteemed for its efficacy in removing rheumatick [sic] complaints. It burns well in lamps and might be advantageously used in lighting streets. If, by some process, it could be rendered inodorus, it would become an important article for domestick [sic] illumination.

Alden's words proved prophetic. By 1830, considerable quantities of "Seneca oil" were reaching New York for medicinal purposes. In the 1840s, Samuel M. Kier of Tarentum, Allegheny County, Pennsylvania, found oil in his salt wells and sold it as medicine. When oil from the salt wells leaked into a nearby canal and caught fire, Kier and others deduced that this oil could be burned in lamps as an illuminant. By 1848, people in Tarentum were lighting their homes with it in spite of the fact that it produced a terrible odor and a considerable amount of smoke. Kier—ever the businessman—concluded that oil could be sold as both a medicine and as an illuminant, provided that it could be clarified in some way. He took a sample of oil to a chemist in Philadelphia, who suggested distilling it but offered no suggestions as to the apparatus that would be required. Kier did some experimenting and, in 1853, opened a refinery on Grant Street in Pittsburgh for the distilling of oil. At first, he operated a one-barrel still—enlarging it later to a five-barrel still. He moved the five-barrel still to Lawrenceville, which was outside the city limits (the city fathers had decided that they did not want such a dangerous operation taking place within their town).

After Kier began refining oil, it was used in the Pittsburgh area for illuminating purposes. Kier then invented a lamp burner which he also put on sale in Pittsburgh.

The market for petroleum as an illuminant was greatly increased after 1857. A. C. Ferris, a New York businessman, visited Pittsburgh that year and, in the basement of a drug store, saw a tin lamp burning carbon oil. Impressed by its possibilities,

Ferris secured a contract with MacKeown and Finley, a Pittsburgh firm that had been distilling oil, to supply him with 2,000 barrels a year. He also purchased some oil from Kier and adapted a lamp that would burn carbon oil.

Ferris' sale of illuminating oil soon outran the supply. The price of oil jumped from 75 cents per gallon to $1.50. All efforts to increase supply failed until Dr. Francis Beattie Brewer, a graduate of Dartmouth College and a practicing physician, moved to Titusville, Crawford County, Pennsylvania, to join his father's lumber firm, Brewer, Watson, and Company. He immediately became interested in an old oil spring located on the company's property two miles below Titusville, near Oil Creek. A thorough examination of this spring and the rest of Oil Creek convinced Dr. Brewer that the oil had great possibilities and should be used.

In the fall of 1853, Dr. Brewer carried a small bottle of petroleum with him on a trip to Hanover, New Hampshire. While there, Dr. Dixi Crosby of the Dartmouth Medical School and Professor O. P. Hubbard of the Chemistry Department of Dartmouth College examined the sample and proclaimed it valuable. However, because it could not be obtained in large quantities, they said that it could hardly become an article of commerce. A few weeks later, George H. Bissell, another graduate of Dartmouth and a lawyer in New York City, saw the bottle of petroleum in Crosby's office and became interested in it. He wondered why petroleum could not be used as an illuminant.

Aroused by the prospect, Bissell and his business partner, Jonathan G. Eveleth, decided that if they could find a good supply of petroleum, they would organize a company, buy the land, develop the spring, and market the petroleum. On November 30, 1854, Bissell and Eveleth purchased from Brewer, Watson and Company of Titusville for $5,000 the Hibbard farm, on which the principal petroleum springs in northwestern Pennsylvania were located. They organized the Pennsylvania Rock Oil Company of New York a month later. This was the first petroleum company in the world. However, because of hard times they found it difficult to sell stock. In April, 1855, Professor Benjamin Silliman, Jr., of Yale College, whom the promoters had hired to analyze the oil, made his report in which he noted its economic value. This proved to be a turning point in the establishment of the petroleum industry.

A number of New Haven capitalists were impressed by Silliman's report and agreed to buy stock, provided that the company was reorganized under the liberal corporation laws of Connecticut. This prompted Eveleth and Bissell to abandon their original enterprise and instead form the Pennsylvania Rock Oil Company of Connecticut on September 18, 1855, with a capital stock of $300,000. The original company sold the Hibbard farm to the new company.

Little progress was made until Bissell saw a bottle of Kier's rock oil in a drugstore window in New York City. He conceived the idea of drilling for petroleum, as Kier had drilled for salt. He persuaded Lyman and Havens, prominent Wall Street real investment brokers, to lease the Hibbard farm and drill for oil. Before they could begin, however, the Panic of 1857 overwhelmed them. Taking advantage of a technicality, they surrendered their lease. James M. Townsend, now president of the Pennsylvania Rock Oil Company, decided that he and his New Haven associates should organized a company, assume the lease, drill for oil and monopolize the oil business. They formed the Seneca Oil Company on March 23, 1858, and with a capital of $300,000 leased the Titusville property from the Pennsylvania Rock Oil Company of Connecticut. Edwin L. Drake was elected General Agent and sent to Titusville in the spring of 1858 to drill for oil.

After many unavoidable delays and after overcoming numerous obstacles, Drake began drilling in the summer of 1859. On a Saturday afternoon, August 27, as Drake and his men were about to quit work, the drill dropped into a crevice at a depth of 69 feet. They then pulled out their tools and went home without any thought of having struck oil. Late Sunday afternoon, the driller, William A. Smith, visited the well, peered into the pipe and saw a dark fluid floating on top of the water. Oil had been struck! Drake had demonstrated a way to secure oil in great abundance. He had tapped the vast subterranean deposits of petroleum underneath the Oil Creek Valley, and—unknown to him at the time—had ushered in a new industry which provided the world with not only a safe and cheap illuminant but also

News of Drake's accomplishment spread rapidly. Within 24 hours, hundreds of people were milling around the Drake Well. An eyewitness wrote that the excitement was fully equal to what he had seen in California at the time of the gold rush. Everyone was wild to lease or buy land and drill a well. Because of the location of the Drake Well, the most attractive land was in the lowlands and as near as possible to the flowing waters of Oil Creek. Consequently, there was a mad rush to secure land near the Drake Well and along the creek. Bissell bought all the stock of the Pennsylvania Rock Oil Company that he could buy and then hurried to Titusville. He boldly leased or purchased farm after farm along Oil Creek and along the Allegheny River (Oil Creek enters the Allegheny at Oil City, Venango County).

Land bordering Oil Creek was soon taken and, within a short time, the entire valley—even far back into the hillsides—had been either leased or purchased. Col. Drake was advised to join the rush to purchase or lease land, but he rejected all counsel. When several other wells were struck, he realized his mistake, but by then it was too late. He ceased to be a factor in the oil industry. Others came in to take advantage of his achievement.

William Barnsdall and Moone Meade of Titusville and Henry Rouse, a merchant from Enterprise, drilled the second well on the Parker farm a short distance above the Drake Well. In November they struck oil but since the yield proved to be less than five barrels daily, they resumed drilling. A few days later, when it was down 112 feet, oil rushed to the top and flowed over the pipe at the rate of about 10 barrels per day. Barnsdall's Well, as they called it, soon became the center of attention and the "lion of the valley."

On the opposite side of Oil Creek from Drake Well and about a mile below, David Crossley of Titusville started drilling the third well. He struck oil March 14, 1860. With a pump it produced 75 to 80 barrels. Thomas A. Gate of Riceville declared:

A splendid thing is the Crossley Well! A diamond of the first order! Enough of itself to silence the cry of humbug, to create a sensation of rival interests or inspire hope in many toiling for subterranean treasure, and to make every son of Pennsylvania rejoice in the good Providence that has enriched the state, not only with vast mines of iron and coal but also with rivers of oil!"

The oil rush was on! Hundreds of people poured into Titusville daily, but by no means was the excitement confined solely to the area around that community. Simultaneously with the drilling of the Barnsdall Well, Brewer, Watson, and Company started putting down a well on the McClintock farm at the lower end of Oil Creek and, in November 1859, they struck oil. By the summer of 1860, at least 12 wells were underway in that area. E.E. Evans, a blacksmith in Franklin, cleaned out an old salt well near that community and, when he struck oil, his well came in at the rate of a barrel an hour. This and another successful drilling venture stimulated a frenzy of drilling activity near Franklin. By August 1860, over 100 wells were being drilled within a mile of the center of Franklin.

And up the Allegheny River, at Tidioute, the excitement over new wells was at fever pitch by August 1860. Oil speculators overran the town, everyone seemed half crazy and according to the *Warren Mail*, it seemed as though half of Warren's population had gathered at Tidioute. The town had three hotels and each had three times as many guests as they could comfortably accommodate.

The production of the pioneer wells in 1859 amounted to about 2,000 barrels but, by the end of 1860, a remarkable change had occurred. By that time there were 74 producing wells, most along Oil Creek. Production amounted to 200,000 barrels for the year. All this production had an effect on price. In 1859, oil sold for 75 cents a gallon. By the end of the year, the price had dropped as low as 22 cents a gallon.

The pioneer wells of 1859 and 1860 produced more oil than anyone had ever seen, but they were nothing compared to the wells began producing in 1861.

A.B. Funk, a lumberman from Warren County, Pennsylvania, completed a well in May 1861 on the David McElhenny farm, seven miles south of Titusville. It began flowing at the rate of 300 barrels per day. Skeptics called it the "Oil Creek humbug" and expected the flow would soon cease, but they waited in vain. It continued flowing for 15 months, then suddenly quit and never produced another barrel, but no matter, by that time it had earned $2,500,000 for Funk (he had paid $1,500 for the farm in 1859).

The Empire Well on the same farm and near the Funk Well, completed in September 1861, flowed at the rate of 3,000 barrels per day! Unable to secure barrels, the owners tried unsuccessfully to check the flow. They built an enclosure around the well, but the oil refused to be dammed and flowed into Oil Creek. The creek was covered with the resultant oil skim for miles. The yield from this well simply bewildered the owners. This well was too productive. With the market already glutted, this well was adding 3,000 barrels a day to the supply. The Empire Well drove the price down to 10 cents a barrel.

Within a few weeks after the Empire started flowing, it was eclipsed by a new well on the James Tarr farm at the lower end of Oil Creek. William Phillips, a salt well driller from the Pittsburgh area, had secured a lease on this farm and, during the summer of 1861, started drilling. He drilled two successful wells of which the second produced 4,000 barrels daily. The flow was so great the owners built underground wooden tanks in which to store the oil. In time these tanks covered several acres.

About four rods away N.S. Woodford drilled another well which began flowing 1,500 barrels per day in July 1862. Water from this well soon flooded Phillips No. 2 and materially reduced the flow of oil from the latter. A peculiar condition developed where neither well would produce oil unless both were pumped at the same time. The owners thus negotiated an agreement whereby both wells were pumped simultaneously and each would get one-third of the production of the other well.

South of the Tarr farm was the Blood farm and to the west the Story farm, both of which developed flowing wells. In 1861 the Blood farm had 12 wells, some of which were very heavy producers. The Story farm had been purchased for $40,000 by some Pittsburghers who later organized into a joint stock company. Andrew Carnegie was was of the principal stockholders in this firm, the Columbia Oil Company. Dividends from oil helped Carnegie erect his new steel mills.

Because of these new wells, production jumped to 5,000 barrels per day in 1861. This was both good and bad. Faced with a fabulous supply but only limited demand, the price of oil fell rapidly. By the end of the year, oil was selling for 10 cents a barrel.

The owners of pumping wells were the most discouraged. Those with wells pumping 5 to 25 barrels per day were disheartened when an adjoining well sprouted hundreds of barrels, flooding the market and making the operation of pumping wells unprofitable. Faced with economic crisis, some of the landowners and operators of wells met at Rouseville (just north of Oil City, Pennsylvania) on November 14, 1861, to organize and take measures to improve the price of oil. They formed the "Oil Creek Association," decided that an inspector should be elected to regulate the production of flowing wells, that oil should not be sold for less than 10 cents per gallon, and that the proceeds should be paid into a general treasury, where it would be held for the order of the seller—less a certain percentage. By January 1862, this first great combination of producers had been organized. They refused to sell oil below $4 a barrel.

Since the price of oil remained low during the first half of 1862, operators of limited means were either ruined or forced to sell. Production fell from 7,000 barrels to 4,000. This decline, coupled with increased use of oil at home and abroad, drove prices up again. By the end of the year oil was selling at $4 a barrel. The condition of the producers improved. It was not necessary to have a very large flowing well to reap a fortune.

At this time Orange Noble and George B. Delamater, merchants from Townville, struck oil on the Farrell farm. Their well, a gusher, sprayed oil and water 100 feet into the air when it came in, enveloping the derrick and nearby trees in a dense spray. The gas flowed like a hurricane, the ground shook and oil flowed at the rate of 3,000 barrels. For days oil flowed into the creek. Men wearing goggles and rubber blankets eventually attached a stopcock that brought it under control. With oil at $4 a barrel and steadily increasing, Noble and Delamater's daily receipts varied from $12,000 to $45,000. Their well flowed for 18 months and netted the owners over $5 million. Their total expenditures for the lease, drilling machinery, and labor amounted to only $4,000. Thus, every dollar they invested netted them a profit of over $15,000!

Although new wells added to the production, the amount of oil produced during the first part of 1863 decreased materially. By that time few new wells were being drilled, production from the older, larger wells was falling off and the small wells pumped only 10 to 60 barrels per day. Besides, Lee's invasion of Pennsylvania in June caused such an excitement that there was almost a total suspension of business in the oil fields for several days. With a decline in production and an increase in demand, the price soared. Oil reached $7.25 a barrel in September and buyers swarmed all over the region.

Up to this point the drilling activity had been confined to the lowlands. In 1864, this changed. Two employees of the Humboldt Refinery at Plumer conceived the daring idea of drilling on land far removed from Oil Creek. In the spring of 1864 they leased 65 acres of the Thomas Holmden farm, located on an upland plateau, 5½ miles from the creek. People thought these two men were insane. They formed the United States Petroleum Company and selected their first drilling site by dowsing with a twig of witchhazel. Their well was spudded in late 1864 and was dubbed the Frazier well.

Before the well was finished, Thomas G. Duncan and George G. Prather bought the Holmden farm, subject to the lease, for $25,000. On January 7, 1865, the Frazier Well began to flow at 250 barrels a day. Stock in the U.S. Petroleum Company jumped from $6.25 to $40 a share.

Excitement in the oil region was intense and drilling for another well was begun. In April 1865 a Boston company completed a well, known as the Homestead Well, just 100 feet outside the boundary of the Holmden farm. It also flowed at the rate of 250 barrels. This prompted the region's wildest oil boom. The U.S. Petroleum Company divided its property into half-acre leases and sold more than 80 of them at an average of $3,000 each. At this same time the production of the Homestead Well suddenly jumped to 500 barrels and the Frazier to 1,200. Excitement was at fever pitch and the leases doubled in price.

A town that became famous in American industrial history, Pithole, was established nearby in May 1865. So great was the speculative fever that four months later it had a population of 15,000 and had the third largest post office in Pennsylvania.

On June 17, the United States Company completed its second well. It flowed 800 barrels a day. Two days later a third well just above the original started flowing 400 barrels. By the end of June 1865, the wells along Pithole Creek were producing 2,000 barrels a day—or one-third the total production of the oil region of 6,000 barrels, which was the total oil production in all the world at that time.

Many factors fueled the Pithole oil boom. The end of the Civil War found the country flooded with paper currency whose holders were anxious to invest and make more money. Thousands of soldiers had been discharged from the army. Many wanted jobs, others wanted to make a fortune quickly after having spent long months on Army pay. The speculative bubble of 1864 and 1865 was at its peak. Hundreds of newly organized companies were ready to lease or buy land wherever there was even a promise of oil. Fired by these circumstances, the Pithole Creek became spectacular.

In Pithole City land could not be bought—only leased for three years with the privilege of removing the buildings when the lease expired or selling them to the owner of the land. If a five-year lease was desired, improvements and buildings had to be surrendered at the end. Most of the lots were leased quickly at the rate of $275 a year. When the frenzy was at its height, these leases were selling for $850—and these were for lots that were only 33 feet wide.

The surrounding forests disappeared quickly as the trees were cut for lumber to build the emerging boom town. The pace of construction was furious. Sometimes men entered into contracts to build a two-story building and had it completed and ready for occupancy within five days. This made for extremely flimsy construction. There was not one brick or stone building erected in all of Pithole.

At its height, Pithole had two banks, two telegraph offices, a daily newspaper, water works system, fire companies, two church buildings, scores of boarding houses, grocery stores, hardware stores, machine shops, and other businesses. There were more than 50 hotels. The Chase Hotel was considered the best. Painted a nut brown color, it cost $80,000 and had a frontage of 180 feet. It could accommodate 200 guests and seat 100 in its dining room. One of the hotel's attractions was its salon, 65 feet long and 28 feet deep "furnished with a luxurious bar and hung with pictures." Murphy's Theater, the largest building in Pithole, had a seating capacity of 1,000.

In addition to these elegant establishments there were numerous brothels, which catered to every variety of taste, pocketbook, and social status. Every other building was a saloon, and every other man was a soldier—Confederate as well as Union. Every day at noon there was a scene unique to Pithole—the daily prostitute parade. Every day, 30 to 40 of the town's ladies of the night mounted horses and rode down the streets, garbed in their best high-necked gowns, hats, and gloves. The men lining the route respected this elegant display by doffing their hats and refrained from making raucous comments or whistling.

Drinking water was scarce. Much profit was made by persons who hauled water in and sold it for 10 cents a glass. As a result, saloons flourished. "Whiskey is cheaper to drink and a lot safer," observed one resident.

If Pithole's rise was phenomenal, its fall was even more rapid. As oil production declined and parts of the town burned to the ground, the exodus from Pithole began. By the end of 1867 the town was, for all practical purposes, dead. That portion of the Holmden farm which at the height of the boom changed hands for $2,000,000 was bought by the Venango County Commissioners for $4.37 in 1878.

Creating a Market for Petroleum

It was Col. Drake himself who was the first oil marketer. Having discovered a rich supply of petroleum, he contracted in 1859 with Sam Kier of Tarentum to supply the latter with oil. Kier in turn promised to sell the oil in preference to any other that should come on the market, but should oil from other sources appear on the market, the price paid by Kier to Drake was to be reduced. Under this arrangement Drake shipped almost $3,800 worth of oil to Kier and over $5,000 worth to W. MacKeown, another oil distiller in Pittsburgh.

Ferris, the New York petroleum dealer, wanted MacKeown to enlarge his distilling plant and take in the product of Brewer and Watson's Well on the McClintock farm, which was then yielding about 20 barrels a day. The officers of the Seneca Oil Company expressed an interest in this plan and offered to sell to Ferris all oil they had to spare, if a satisfactory price could be agreed upon, and they agreed not to distill or sell to others. In return, they wanted Ferris and MacKeown to distill all the oil the Seneca people sold them. Under this arrangement, the Seneca people would control the crude oil and MacKeown and Ferris the refined. MacKeown's reluctance to accept this offer scuttled this plan.

In order to introduce his product and solicit orders, Drake made a trip in February 1860 to Erie, Chicago, Cincinnati, and Pittsburgh; but he, as well as the New Haven stockholders, found oil difficult to sell. Some machinists recommended it highly as a lubricant; others were afraid the oil would injure their machinery, and they objected to the odor.

While in Pittsburgh, Drake met George M. Mowbray, a chemist associated with the wholesale drug firm of Schieffelins Brothers and Company of New York. Mowbray saw the value of oil, and the two men struck a contract under which Drake agreed to ship to Schieffelins all the oil except what was already obligated from the wells of the Seneca Oil Company. In turn, Schieffelins guaranteed all sales, agreed to return all proceeds after deducting the charges, and for this service, they were to receive a commission of 7½ percent.

Although Drake had negotiated outlets through Kier, MacKeown, and Schieffelins, the chief difficulty in trying to sell petroleum was its disagreeable odor, its impurities, and its dark, muddy color. Petroleum needed to be deodorized, decolored and purified before it could be sold extensively, but there were no refineries except the small ones of Kier, MacKeown, and Ferris. The Seneca Oil Company decided to go into the refining business, but internal dissension and bankruptcy prevented them from doing so.

Nevertheless, after the completion of the Drake Well, refineries sprung up almost instantaneously along Oil Creek and the Allegheny River, at Union Mills, Corry, and Erie. W. H. Abbott, James Parker, and William Barnsdall built the first refinery in Titusville in the fall of 1860. A large part of the machinery and appliances, purchased in Pittsburgh, were shipped up the Allegheny by boat to Oil City, thence up Oil Creek. When completed, the refinery consisted of six stills and bleachers, with all the tanks and fixtures under one roof. The first run of oil was made on January 22, 1861. The yield did not exceed 50 percent of the crude. Not knowing how to utilize the byproducts, they were either dumped into Oil Creek or all the tar and naphtha were burned.

At the upper end of Cherry Run, near Plumer (just a few miles from Oil Creek), John E. Bruns and the Ludovici brothers of New York City erected the Humboldt Refinery in 1862. The plant covered several acres, employed 200 men, and was the largest in the oil region at the time. Its owners shipped a large portion of their product to Europe, where they had extensive connections.

The most famous of all the early refineries was the Samuel D. Downer plant at Corry. That location was picked because it was at the junction of the Philadelphia & Erie and the Atlantic & Great Western railroads. Construction began in October 1861. When completed, Downer could refine 400 barrels of oil daily. Over 150 men were employed. Downer proved to be an important factor in the marketing of petroleum.

The number of refineries rapidly increased. The oil region had 15 refineries in 1860; by 1863 there were 61. Pittsburgh, which became the earliest refining center because of its location on the Allegheny River, had five large refineries in 1860. By 1863 it had 60, representing a capital investment of $1 million, employed 600 men and had a total weekly capacity of 26,000 barrels.

Simultaneously with the expansion of the home market, petroleum was introduced to Europe. In 1860, the officers of the Seneca Oil Company sent samples to A. Gelee, a French chemist. After analyzing it, Gelee said, "If that oil can be gathered in quantity enough, its illuminating and lubricating qualities are such that for these purposes it will revolutionize the world."

Although many Europeans saw its advantages, others—particularly the manufacturers of coal oil—had strong prejudices against it. These manufacturers feared that this new American product would put them out of business. It did. By 1862, the *Times* of London predicted that the value of the oil trade might approach that of American cotton. Europeans found it was a better and cheaper illuminant than olive oil. In 1862, oil was introduced into Russia. By 1863, the use of kerosene in lamps far exceeded that of tallow. "The people are becoming accustomed to it," reported the United States Consul at St. Petersburg in December 1863. By the end of the Civil War, oil had become America's sixth leading export, exceeded only by gold, corn, tobacco, wheat, and wheat flour.

Improvements in refining methods were made regularly. In 1860 to 1961 Luther Atwood of the Downer organization introduced preheating. H. P. Gengembre of Pittsburgh introduced it differently. Atwood piped superheated steam into the still while Gengembre sent preheated oil into the still. Outside the oil country, Giuseppe Tagliabue invented the flash and fire closed-cup method to enable refiners to determine the temperature at which oil makes enough vapor to form an explosive mixture with air. Joshua Merrill was the first to use sulfuric acid and alkali as a deodorizing and bleaching agent. In 1869, he discovered by accident how to refine an oil of heavy viscosity. He did it by carefully controlling the temperature so that refining could take place without the oil decomposing or "cracking."

By 1863, refineries located further from the oil producing region had increased to the point where their combined capacity exceeded 28,000 barrels per day. The New York City area had a capacity of 9,790, Baltimore had 1,098, Boston 3,500, but the biggest of all was the Cleveland area, which had a capacity of 12,732 barrels per day.

In other parts of the nation, refiners also made important contributions toward refining skills. In 1866, Hiram Everest introduced the vacuum still at Rochester, New York, using lower temperatures that prevent cracking or decomposition. To handle crude oils containing sulfur, Herman Frasch in 1886 introduced metallic oxide to solve the problem of sulfur removal.

As refining methods improved, new products were introduced. Lighter naphthas served as solvents, cleaning agents, and turpentine substitutes; gasoline was employed in air-gas engines as early as 1863; liquified petroleum gases were discovered in 1866 and used in medicine and in compression machines used to make ice. Paraffin wax and petrolatum (petroleum jelly) were also valuable byproducts.

Transporting petroleum to market was very difficult at first. Oil Creek itself served as the original means of transportation. Oil was loaded on flatboats and floated downstream, but highwater stages occurred only six months out of the year. The rest of the time, the oilmen utilized the pond freshet—a method loggers had used for years to float their logs downstream.

To create the pond freshet, there were at least 17 sawmills with dams on the principal branches of Oil Creek. Through a system of floodgates, the water flow could be halted until a sufficient quantity was backed up, then it was released to create a swell of water big enough to float the logs downstream. As the pond freshet passed, the cuts in the dams were closed and the water was held again until enough logs had been sawed to warrant another freshet.

The oilmen saw immediately this could become a viable method for them to get their oil downstream. Accordingly, they struck deals with the sawmill operators for use of their dams. The latter charged fees which increased as the demands for water by the oilmen became more frequent.

During the busy season, pond freshets were provided twice a week. The superintendent set the date and notified shippers and boatmen well in advance so that they could overhaul their flatboats and tow them to a point on the creek to be loaded. The boats were of all sizes and kinds, and most could hold 700 to 800 barrels. They carried the oil either in bulk or in barrels.

A cool breeze was the first sign of the freshet's approach and the swirling waters soon followed. Expectant boatmen stood ready to cast off their lines when the current was precisely right. Inexperienced boatmen generally cut their boats loose too soon. Their boats became grounded and were battered into kindling by those coming later. An experienced boatman waited until the water began to recede, then cut his lines loose, throwing himself onto the mercy of a swift current.

On each freshet there were 150 to 200 flatboats, all loaded with oil either in barrels or in bulk, floating endways or sideways, all trying to wind their way down Oil Creek, a stream that was only 12 rods wide and very crooked as it wound its way past steep hills. It required boatmen of considerable skill to avoid collisions with other boats, rocks, and other obstructions. If a boat was crosswise on the creek, a jam often occurred. The boats, built of light timber, were easily crushed and the oil spilled into the creek. If the oil was in barrels, the boat sank, the barrels floated off, and the owner rarely recovered all of them.

If the boats successfully passed these obstacles, they still had to get to Oil City where Oil Creek emptied into the Allegheny. The cry of "pond freshet" brought out the entire population of the town; it was a gala occasion. Crowds gathered on the shores to watch. Even here, however, the boatmen were not out of danger. Often a boat struck a rock a few rods above the Oil City bridge; others struck the piers of the bridge itself. In either case, the boats were usually rendered into kindling and the oil lost.

Oil lost from the overturned boats floated into the eddies below the mouth of Oil Creek and belonged to whoever dipped it up. Oil was so plentiful after one of these disasters that people leased land between Oil City and Franklin for the purpose of throwing out booms and taking up the oil as it went downstream.

In November 1861, Jacob Jay Vandergrift of Pittsburgh started the bulk oil boat business when he towed two large coal boats loaded with 4,000 empty barrels to Oil City with his steamer, the Red Fox. While delivering the barrels, he bought 5,000 barrels worth of oil, then he had to figure out a way to get all that oil back to Pittsburgh. His solution: he had a contractor build 12 boats that were 80 feet long, 14 feet wide, and three feet deep, each with a capacity of 400 barrels. With these boats, Vandergrift launched a very profitable barge business. These boats were the precursors of today's huge tankers.

During the warm summer months, water transportation was not feasible—Oil Creek and the Allegheny River were too low. During these months, oil had to be hauled overland. Prior to 1862, the nearest railroad stations to the oil region were those at Corry, Union Mills (now Union City), and Garland—each about 25 miles north of Titusville. Getting oil to these railroad stations was an undertaking of garguantan proportions. As many as 6,000 teamsters were regularly engaged in hauling oil by horse-drawn wagon. It was reported that as many as 2,000 teams passed over the Franklin Street bridge in Titusville in just one day. It was not uncommon to see a solid line of teams a mile or more in length on the roads leading to Union Mills, Corry, and Garland.

All this travel was done on roads which were, to say the least, muddy. Oil leaking from the barrels on the wagons mixed with the mud, creating a gooey paste which destroyed the capillary glands and hair of the horses. This meant most of these horses had no hair below the neck. The mud was so thick that many wagons dropped into mudholes below their axles, horses sank to their bellies, and many of them— falling into the muddy morass—were simply left to smother. Hundreds of horses could be seen along the banks of Oil Creek. If this happened, the teamster driver simply secured another horse, but in doing so, he lost his place in the line. He therefore had to take his place at the end. If a wagon broke down, the driver dumped the load onto the ground and went on, leaving the oil to be stolen by anyone who thought it valuable enough to be worth taking.

In 1862, all this changed with the coming of the railroad. Shortly after Drake's discovery, a group of capitalists headed by Thomas Struthers of Warren, Pennsylvania, organized and capitalized the Oil Creek Railroad. Its charter authorized this company to construct a railroad from any point along the Philadelphia & Lake Erie Railroad to Titusville, thence along Oil Creek to Oil City and Franklin. In 1862 this company built a line from Corry to Titusville. Corry was selected as the northern terminus in order to connect with both the Philadelphia & Lake Erie and the Atlantic & Great Western Railroad, which also served that community. Within two years the Oil Creek Railroad had also constructed a line from Titusville south along Oil Creek to the Shaffer farm.

From the beginning, the Oil Creek Railroad had an overwhelming amount of business. During its first 14 months of existence, it carried 430,684 barrels of oil, 459,424 empty barrels, 22,727 tons of merchandise, and 59,987 passengers.

The Atlantic & Great Western Railroad, having captured a large portion of the oil sent east from Corry, became interested in gaining control of the oil shipped from the southern end of the oil region, at Franklin. Accordingly, it extended a line from Corry to Meadville and thence to Franklin, completing it by March 1865.

The hold of the teamsters on the oil transportation business was also shaken by Samuel Van Syckel, the man who built the first successful oil pipeline from Pithole to Miller Farm on Oil Creek in 1865. This line extended for 5½ miles and utilized two-inch pipe. Capacity of the line was 1,500 barrels per day. A tank farm with the capacity for holding 20,000 barrels of oil was constructed on the Miller farm. Four 10-horsepower engines were used to pipe the oil over the hills between Pithole and Miller farm. Oil from the pipeline was placed into the tanks. Large platforms were built adjacent to the railroad, upon which barrels were filled by means of pipes extending from the tanks. The filled barrels were then rolled onto railroad cars.

By the mid-1860s much of the oil drilling activity was centered around Wildcat Hollow and Petroleum Center, an oil town that sprung up in the very center of the oil region. Wildcat Hollow—an almost circular ravine of half bowl facing Oil Creek—was purchased by Frederick Prentice of New York City in 1863. Prentice had recently formed the New Jersey Oil Company. His partners were James Bishop, then a resident of New Brunswick, New Jersey, and George Bissell, then a resident of Franklin, Pennsylvania. This trio together formed the Central Petroleum Company of New York City and began drilling. They took a new approach—they began drilling in previously unknown territory (i.e., Wildcat Hollow). From this is derived a term still used today, "wildcatters." Their efforts proved fabulously successful. Nearly 200 wells were drilled in Wildcat Hollow, some so productive that the area became a center for early refining activity. At one time seven refineries were located in the Hollow. One of these was the Monitor Oil Works which was owned partly by George Stephens. Stephens later moved into Titusville, where he invested in other refineries, lumber mills, stave mills and a barrel factory which he owned jointly with Michael Heisman, father of college football coach John Heisman (1869–1936) for whom the Heisman trophy is named.

The Central Petroleum Company established a town called Petroleum Center on the lands adjacent to Wildcat Hollow. Petroleum Center reached its peak during the years 1866 to 1870. It was known for its spectacular oil wells and also for crime including gambling, prostitution, drunkenness and murder.

President Ulysses S. Grant visited Petroleum Center by train on September 14, 1871. Grant made a speech at the Central House and made stops at Columbia Farm, Tarr Farm, Rouseville, and Oil City. This visit proved to be Petroleum Center's swan song. Production declined rapidly after that.

Several methods were used to halt the decline of marginal oil wells. Casing was installed in many producing wells to keep water from ruining oil production. The invention of the Roberts torpedo in 1866 enabled producers to remove paraffin deposits from marginal wells. The Roberts torpedo used nitroglycerin to literally explode the unwanted paraffin away. Suction pumps were used to remove natural gas from the wells. These led eventually to the development of the natural gas industry.

No discussion of oil industry history is complete without mention of John D. Rockefeller. In 1860, Rockefeller—then a young produce merchant from Cleveland, Ohio—visited Titusville to look into the oil business. When he returned home, he reported that he felt the oil business was uncertain from the producing standpoint, but that the refining aspect of the industry looked promising if a continuing supply of crude oil could be obtained. He bought a small refinery in Cleveland two years later, but in 1865, when he learned of the discovery of oil in the Pithole field, he became assured there would be a good supply of oil for many years. He therefore bought out his partner in the oil business. Within a short time he was making his own barrels, making acids, buying crude directly from the producers and hauling much of his oil with his own horses and wagons.

Rockefeller thrived, but he and the other Cleveland producers were hampered by their location. They had to haul oil in from Western Pennsylvania to be processed in Cleveland, and then had to ship it back to the East Coast markets by rail. In the spring of 1868, to reduce his transportation costs, Rockefeller approached the Lake

Shore Railroad branch of the New York Central system and demanded a rebate on all oil shipped. To gain leverage, he threatened to move his refineries from Cleveland into the oil region if the rebate was not granted. The railroad went along and granted a rebate on crude oil and on kerosene transshipped to New York. It should be noted that rebates were common in those days. Rockefeller simply applied the rebate method to a field where it had never been tried before. It worked. By 1869 Rockefeller's refineries were the largest in the world and he proudly proclaimed, "The oil business is mine."

By the early 1870s, the oil industry was very unpredictable. Production often exceeded demand, and when railroads and pipelines could not move all the crude being produced, storage tanks filled quickly and eventually prices fell. The market was, in a word, cyclical. The producers tried several times to control production in order to stabilize the market, but they met with little success.

The refiners were in an even more precarious position. By 1871, refining capacity was more than double the production of crude. Refiners found themselves bidding against each other to obtain crude in order to keep their refineries operating. Naturally, few refineries operated at full capacity and some were forced to close.

The largest refiners—most importantly, Rockefeller—and the railroads were especially concerned, and they did something about it. A clandestine organization of an abandoned Pennsylvania corporation, the South Improvement Company, was effected January 18, 1872, when a secret contact and agreement was accepted by the chief officers of the New York Central, Erie, and Pennsylvania Railroads and by 13 of the largest refiners from Cleveland, Pittsburgh, and New York. When news of this secret agreement became known, 20 of the 25 independent refiners in Cleveland sold out to the Rockefeller group (Standard Oil of Ohio) in less than six weeks.

The South Improvement Company agreement split oil freight on a percentage basis among the three railroads. These roads agreed to double rates on crude oil and refined oil from the oil regions to the refining centers, promised members of the Company a maximum rebate of 50 percent, agreed to furnish waybills on all oil shipped over their lines to members of the Company, and introduced the "drawback," whereby members of the South Improvement Company received rebates on oil shipped by their competitors.

The plot was accidentally revealed on February 25, 1872, when an employee of the Jamestown & Franklin Division of the Lake Shore Railroad raised the rates prematurely. The independent refiners and producers were furious. They faced ruin and the loss of huge investments. Mass meetings were held at Tidioute, Erie, and Shamburg. On February 27, 1872, 3,000 furious oilmen met at Titusville's Parshall Opera House to give battle to the combination. On March 1, under the leadership of Captain William Hasson, John Archbold, and Jacob J. Vandergrift, a Petroleum Producers Association was formed, pledges were made that no wells would be drilled for 60 days, and crude was to be sold only to those refiners who were not connected with the South Improvement Company. New York and Baltimore producers soon joined with the Pennsylvania independents. They contacted the state legislature, and on April 2, 1872, the charter of the South Improvement Company was revoked by the state.

The victory of the independents seemed complete, but the very next month Rockefeller and his aides formed a new association called the Petroleum Refiners

Association, of which he was president. This new unincorporated association was open to any and all refiners who would place themselves under the control of a central board. The board would handle crude oil purchases, allocate refining quotas, fix prices, and negotiate freight rates with the railroads.

The independent producers, skeptical of the plan and alarmed because of increasing production from Armstrong, Butler, and Clarion Counties in Pennsylvania, formed the Petroleum Producers Agency to buy and, if necessary, hold the crude in storage at $5 a barrel, cut production, and build refineries. Rockefeller recognized this new danger and offered to purchase their crude if production could be controlled. The producers signed with Rockefeller, but drilling and new production in the new fields ran rampant. The new joint agreement was eventually canceled.

Through these two failures, Rockefeller learned that loose combinations could not properly control either production or refining. He therefore took more positive steps. First, he secured from the Erie Railroad both barreling and shipping facilities in New Jersey, thus enabling him to control the export end of the market. Next, he persuaded the railroads handling the oil traffic to equalize the rates on crude oil and kerosene. Then, he hired Daniel O'Day to head his American Transfer Company and to build pipelines from the Clarion oil field to Emlenton, where rail connection could be made to Franklin and Cleveland. In 1874 and in 1879, he bought the interests of the largest independent pipelines and, by 1883, he organized the National Transit Company. Takeovers of refineries began in 1874. Refiners not willing to sell out to him were drastically undersold, found themselves without barrels, had delays in securing tank cars and learned that part of the freight rates they paid were rebated to others.

It did not take long for Standard Oil to buy 20 of the 21 refineries in Pittsburgh, 10 of the 12 in Philadelphia, and all of them in the actual oil regions. By July 1878, at the age of 38, Rockefeller controlled 97 percent of all the pipelines and refineries in the country.

Not all the independent Pennsylvania oilmen stood idly by while Standard Oil moved to control every phase of their business. They were aided by the discovery of oil in a new field, the Bradford, Pennsylvania, field. This proved to be a prolific area.

Bradford, in McKean County about 100 miles north and east of Oil Creek, was a sleepy village of 500 people at the beginning of 1875. By year's end, wildcatters had penetrated the oil-bearing sands around the town and a new rush was on. Train loads of oilmen from "the lower country" crowded the streets and overran the hotels. Main Street at night looked like a frontier town. Saloons and dance halls were thronged and gambling dens ran without interference.

By 1878, Bradford had a population of 4,000. Over 1,000 letters were received daily at the post office. The money order business amounted to $2,000 a week. Railroad traffic was tremendous. At times there were as many as 250 loaded cars standing in the yards. With 7,000 producing wells in the region averaging 65,000 barrels a day, Bradford was the oil metropolis of the world in 1880. By then its population exceeded 11,000 and its post office was the third largest in Pennsylvania.

All this new production gave the independent oilmen a tool with which to combat Standard Oil. In 1878, three of Standard's foes—Byron Benson, David K. McKelvy, and Major Robert E. Hopkins—formed the Tidewater Pipe Company.

Financed by many of the largest regional producers, this firm constructed a pipeline from Coryville in the Bradford field to Williamsport. From there, the Reading Railroad took the oil to the sea. The line was started in November 1878 and completed the following spring. It was a godsend to the few independent refineries still in operation in New York and Philadelphia. They were glad to get some relief from Standard Oil pressure and control. The cost of getting a barrel of oil to seaboard via this pipe was 17 cents, compared with the previous price of 85 cents. The heyday of railroad transportation of oil was ending.

The Tidewater independent pipeline was a real threat to Rockefeller's interests, and he reacted in his characteristic manner—he bought out all the refineries that had promised to take oil from Tidewater's pipes, with one exception. Even this did not kill Tidewater, for that firm simply went out and built plants of its own at Philadelphia and Bayonne, New Jersey. Finding no other means of putting the new firm out of business, Rockefeller purchased one-third of Tidewater's stock and, by 1883, Standard Oil and Tidewater ended their battles and became allies.

The independents fought back again. Lewis Emery, Jr., of Bradford, an implacable foe of Standard Oil, organized the United States Pipeline Company and by July 1893 had a crude line extending eastward as well as a refined line from the region's producers.

In January 1895, the producers and refiners who had suffered much from Standard Oil met in Butler, Pennsylvania, and formed the Pure Oil Company. Five years later, Pure Oil merged with Emery's United States Pipeline Company. By 1901, their pipeline had reached Philadelphia and the seaboard.

The struggle of the independent oilmen was long and difficult, but proof of how well they built is evidenced by the fact the Tidewater Oil Company (now known as Getty Oil Company) and Pure Oil (now a division of Union Oil Company) are still important factors in the oil business.

The Sherman Antitrust Act was passed July 2, 1890. In 1911, the Supreme Court ruled that Standard Oil had violated this act and directed that the corporation dissolve itself within six months. As a result, Standard Oil was broken into 34 separate companies.

By the turn of the century, the oil business began to change significantly. First, with the depletion of the Pennsylvania oil fields, the focus of crude oil production shifted westward to California and Texas. Second, with electricity becoming more and more popular as a source of lighting, oil fell out of favor as the primary raw material used for illumination (although its use as a lubricant was still unparalleled). The advent of the automobile, however, changed all that.

The first producing oil well in California was drilled by a Pennsylvanian, Robert McPherson, at Pico Canyon in 1876. By 1890, Lyman Stewart and W. L. Hardison had formed the Union Oil Company and entered the search for oil in the San Fernando Valley. In 1892, Stewart hit a gusher near Los Angeles. This signaled the beginning of the great California oil boom. By 1895, nearly 3,000 wells had been drilled in the Los Angeles oil field. Standard Oil discovered a second oil field at Huntingdon Beach in 1920 and Shell Oil Company found a third at Signal Hill in 1921.

Oil was first discovered in a water well in Texas in 1894. This proved a precursor of things to come. In 1899, Petillo Higgins and Anthony F. Lucas, using the newly invented rotary drilling platform, began to drill at Big Hill near Beaumont, Texas. They drilled for two years without success. Then two Pennsylvanians, John H. Galey and James M. Guffey, began prospecting for oil in this same area. Backed by a $300,000 loan from Pittsburgh banker Andrew Mellon, they took over Galey and Guffey's operation and resumed drilling with new equipment. In 1901, at a depth of 1,000 feet, they struck black gold. Their well in the Spindletop section of Big Hill erupted with a mighty fury. Their Spindletop Well flowed at the rate of 100,000 barrels per day—the largest gusher the world had ever seen. With a year, more than 400 gushers had been drilled at Spindletop. Oil became so plentiful that the price plummeted to three cents per barrel. Lucas, Galey, and Guffey, with Mellon's financing, started the Gulf Refining Company, which later became Gulf Oil Corporation.

A mere 20 miles to the south, Joseph S. Cullinan organized the Texas Company, which later became Texaco. This firm discovered the great Gulf Coast salt domes, which were prolific oil producers. Texaco later joined with Gulf and Sun to create the world's largest oil exporting facility at Port Arthur, Texas. These three firms were soon able to supply the Eastern refineries with more oil in one year than Pennsylvania had in the previous ten.

Although oil was discovered in Oklahoma as early as 1859 (same year as Drake's discovery), Oklahoma's oil boom didn't begin in earnest until 1905 when the 8,000-acre Glenn Pool field near Tulsa was discovered. By 1907 Oklahoma was the top oil producing state. With production at Spindletop falling off, Gulf and Texaco both built pipelines from Port Arthur to the fabulously rich Glenn Pool reserves. At the same time, Standard Oil extended its Atlantic pipeline to Oklahoma.

In 1913, Harry Sinclair tapped an incredible gusher at Cushing, Oklahoma. That town soon became an oil boom town. It was here that the science of petroleum geology was born. Charles N. Gould of the University of Oklahoma discovered that oil was usually found under anticlines (arched ridges of rock located underground). To prove his theory, Gould mapped two oil fields in Kansas in 1915. These fields—Augusta and El Dorado—eventually yielded more than 200 million barrels of oil.

APPENDIX C
Collectors' Resources

Publications

Mobilia
Eric Killorin
Hyatt Research Corp.
P.O. Box 575
Middlebury, VT 05753
(802) 545-2510

WOCCO
Clark Miller
2625 River Rd.
Willoughby, OH 44094
(216) 946-2640

Check The Oil
Jerry Keyser
Box 1000
Westerville, OH 43081

Hemmings Motor News
Box 100
Bennington, VT 05201
(802) 442-3101

Tiger Rag
Villa Publishing Syndicate Inc.
Ed Love
P.O. Box 25763
Colorado Springs, CO 80936
(719) 528-8867

Conventions

Iowa Gas Swap Meet, Inc.
Des Moines, IA 50322
(515) 276-2099

1st Annual Historic Oil Region Oil &
    Gas Convention/1994
Mark Anderton
Oil City, PA 16301
(814) 677-6070

Bibliography

American Association of Petroleum Geologists. *History of the Petroleum Industry Symposium.* The American Association of Petroleum Geologists, 1989.

Anderson, Scott. *Check the Oil: A Pictorial History of the American Filling Station.* Wallace-Homestead Book Company, Lombard, Illinois, 1986.

Anderton, Mark, and Sherry Mullen. *Collectors Auction Services Catalog #6.* Oil City, Pennsylvania, June 1991.

———. *Collectors Auction Services Catalog #7.* Oil City, Pennsylvania, February 1992.

———. *Collectors Auction Services Catalog #8.* Oil City, Pennsylvania, June, 1992.

———. *Collectors Auction Services Catalog #9.* Oil City, Pennsylvania, April, 1993.

Etzel, Judith. "Vestige of Oil Refinery Falls Victim to Progress." *The Derrick.* Oil City, Pennsylvania, November 19, 1992, p. 14.

Giddens, Paul H. *The Birth of the Oil Industry.* Pennsylvania Historical and Museum Commission, 1938.

Giddens, Paul H. *Pennsylvania Petroleum, 1750–1872.* Pennsylvania Historical and Museum Commission, 1947.

Giddens, Paul H. *Early Days of Oil: A Pictorial History of the Beginnings of the Industry in Pennsylvania.* Pennsylvania Historical and Museum Commission, 1948.

Henderson, Wayne, and N. C. Marshall. Telephone interview, April 4, 1993.

Miller, Ernest C. *Pennsylvania's Oil Industry*, 1974.

Mong, Margaret. *Oil Creek and Titusville Railroad Interpretative Manual*, 1988.

Index

Abbot, W. H., 139
Abbreviations, 130
Ace High Motor Oil, 32
AC Service, 84
Advertising, 5
Aero Eastern Motor Oil, 52
Air compressor. *See* Color Plates
Airflite Motor Oil, 48
Air Race Motor Oil, 28
ALA, 78
Alden, Timothy, 142
All American Motor Oil, 49
Allegheny River Valley oil wells, 135–137
AllFire Gasoline, 14
Amalie Motor Oil, 94
American Oil Company, 89, 108
American Coach Oil, 28
American Liberty Oil Company, 14
American Lubricants Incorporated, 41
American Motor Hotel Association, 89
American Transfer Company, 145
AMHA, 89
Amoco. *See* American Oil Company
Anderton, Thomas, 6
Antifreeze containers, 73–74
Archbold, John, 144
Archer Petroleum Corporation, 49
Arm patches, 108–109
Armstrong Rhino-Flex Tires, 78
Around The World Motor Oil, 50
The Arrow Oil Company, 33, 62
Ashtrays, 117
Astrostar Tires, 99
Atlantic & Great Western Railroad, 142
Atlantic Flying A, 110
Atlantic Refining Company, 10, 14, 22, 58, 61, 68, 80, 110, 122
The Atlas Oil Company, 50
Atwood, Luther, 140
Autocrat Motor Oil, 62
Auto-Lite, 83
Auto Lite Spark Plugs, 100
Automobile Club of Pittsburgh, 118
Automobile Gasoline Company, 4
Automobile Legal Association, 78
Automobiles, 1, 2–3
Automotive Maintenance Association Inc., 89

Banks, 122–123
Banners, 86–87
Barnsdall Lubricant, 68
Barnsdall, William, 134, 139
Bayerson Oil Works, 62
Beckett Bros., 58
The Bell Oil and Gas Company, 14, 68
Bellube Grease, 68
Ben Franklin Gasoline, 15
Benz, Karl, 2
B.F. Goodrich, 81, 84
Bibliography, 149
Bishop, James, 143
The Bison Oil Products Co., Inc., 29
Bissell, George H., 133, 134, 143
Blotters, 129
Blue Crown Spark Plugs, 100
Blue Grass Axle Grease. *See* Color Plates
Booster Chemical and Engineering Company, 59
Bowser, Sylvanus F., 4
Boyce Moto Meter, 100
Bradford oil wells, 145–146
Brewer, Dr. Francis Beattie, 133
Bruns, John E., 139
Buick Manufacturing Company, 3
Buss Auto Fuses, 100
Butternut Valley Hardware Company, 80

Cabinets, 100, 101
Cadillac Manufacturing Company, 3
Calendars, 119–121. *See also* Color Plates
California, 2, 146
Calso Gasoline, 110
Cambridge Cars, 87
Canfield Oil Company, 29
Capitan Parlube Motor Oil, 58
Car cleaner containers, 66–67
Cardboard banks, 123
Cardboard signs, 88
Cars, 1, 2–3
Carter CarBUREter, 89. *See also* Color Plates
Casper Brake & Clutch Company, 107
Cato Oil and Grease Company, 33
Cavalier Motor Oil, 59
C.C. Snowdon Oil Refiner and Manufacturer, 47
Central Petroleum Company, 143

Chain store tax, 5
Chalmers-Motor-Car-Co., 87
Champion Spark Plugs, 96, 101, 126
Champlin Gasoline, 15
Chas. F. Kellom and Co., Inc., 36, 39
Chevrolet, 3, 88, 113, 120, 127
Chevron, 108
Chieftain Motor Oil, 33
Christenson Oil Company, 52
Chrysler Motors Parts Corporation, 85
Cigar box, 127
Cigarette lighters, 117
The Cincinnati Advertising Products Co., 18
Citgo, 109
Cities Service, 16, 112
Clipboard, 126
Clocks, 94–95
Coal boats, 141
Columbia Petroleum Products Company, 55
Conoco Inc., 10, 16, 22, 41, 117, 123
Containers
  antifreeze, 73–74
  car cleaner, 66–67
  collectibility of, 65
  engine product, 75–76
  grease, 68–73
  lubricant, 68–73
Continental Oil Company, 2, 10, 16, 22, 41
Continental Refining Company, 6, 56, 62
Cooper Tires, 78, 80
Coreco Motor Oil, 62, 126
Cornell Tire and Rubber Company, 101
Credit card machine, 113
Crew Levick, 41
Crosby, Dr. Dixi, 133
Cross-Country Motor Oil, 43
Crossley, David, 134
Cruiser Motor Oil, 30
Cullinan, Joseph S., 2, 147
Cushing Gasoline, 16

Deep Rock Oil Corporation, 28
Defender Motor Oil, 50
Delamater, George B., 136
Desmonds Miracle Oil, 68
Diamond Gasolene, 17, 19
Dietz, 113

Dietz Ideal Motor Headlamps, 113
Dixie Oils Gasoline, 16
Dodge Trucks, 126
Dorfman Bros., Manufacturers of
    Advertising Thermometers, 97
Double Eagle Lubricants, Inc., 30
Downer, Samuel D., 139
Drake, Col. Edwin L., 1, 131, 132,
    134, 138, 139
Dryden Dieselall Motor Oil, 123
Dryer Clark and Dryer Oil Com-
    pany, 34
Duncan, Thomas G., 137
Durant, William, 3
Dura-Products Manufacturing
    Company, 118
Duryea, Charles, 2
Duryea, Frank, 2
D-X, 17, 118

E & S Motors Sales & Service,
    Inc., 92
Eagle Oil & Supply Company, 51
Easy-pour oil cans, five-gallon,
    62–64. See also Color Plates
Echlin, 113
Edison Mazda Lights, 101
Emery, Louis, Jr., 146
Empire Oil Works, Inc., 41, 64
Empire Well, 135
En-Ar-Co, 29, 43, 59, 69
Engine product containers, 75–76
Engines, 3
Erie Railroad, 145
Esso, 11, 86, 121, 122, 123
Ethyl gasoline, 10, 15, 17, 20, 22
Ethyl Gasoline Corporation, 15
European market, 140
Evans, E.E., 135
Eveleth, Jonathan G., 143
Eveready Prestone Anti-Freeze, 73
Everest, Hiram, 140
Exide Batteries, 79

"Falcon" poster, 88
Farrington Manufacturing Com-
    pany, 113
Ferris, A.C., 132–133, 138–139
Fire Chief Gasoline, 23, 79
Fireman's hat, miniature, 129
Firestone, 80, 83, 94, 101, 120
Fisk, 75, 127
Five-gallon easy-pour oil cans,
    62–64. See also Color Plates
Five-gallon oil cans, 58–61
Five-quart oil cans, 37–41
Flanged signs, 83–85. See also
    Color Plates
Flash and fire closed-cup method,
    140
Flebing Chemical Company, 66
Fleet-Wing Motor Oil, 30
Fleetwood Motor Oil, 48
Flying A, 26, 110, 116. See also At-
    lantic Refining Company;
    Tydol
Ford, Henry, 2
Ford Motor Company, 73, 102
Frazier Well, 137
Freedom Oil Works Company, 31,
    37

Freeman Headbolt Engine Heater,
    96
French Auto Oil, 60
Funk, A.B., 135

Galenol Motor Oil, 44
Galey, John H., 2, 147
Gargoyle, 33, 34, 37, 40
Gas and tax price stand, miniature,
    128
Gas globes, 9, 14–22. See also
    Color Plates
Gasoline, 3–6. See also Oil industry
Gasoline pump nozzle, 13
Gas pumps, 4, 9, 10–14
Gas pump toy, 124
Gas shortages of 1970s, 5
Gas-station collectibles, 6–7. See
    also specific items
Gas stations, 1, 4
Gate, Thomas A., 134
Gelee, A., 140
General Electric, 101
General Motors Corporation, 3
The General Refining Company,
    51
Gengembre, H.P., 140
Germania Refining Company, 96
Getty Oil Company, 1–2, 108,
    146
Giant Power, 87
Gilmer Moulded Rubber Fan Belt,
    103
Giveaways. See Souvenirs
Glasses, 126, 127
Glenn Pool oil field, 2, 147
Globe Gasoline, 18
Golden Leaf Motor Oil, 28
Gold Medal Motor Oils, 97
Gold Star, 90
Goodrich. See B.F. Goodrich
Goodyear, 81, 97
Gould, Charles N., 147
Grading guide, 7
Grand Champion Motor Oil, 54
Grant, Ulysses S., 143
Grate Stuf! Radiator Seal, 75
Grease containers, 68–73
Green Ray Motor Oil, 51
Gree-Soft Automobile Soap, 66
Grey Rock Lubrication, 107
Guffey, James M., 2, 147
Gulf Oil Corporation, 2, 4, 11, 38,
    56, 74, 102, 109, 111, 127,
    147
Gulf Refining Company, 2, 56, 66,
    71, 84, 147. See also Gulf Oil
    Corporation

Half-gallon oil cans, 41–43. See
    also Color Plates
Haney's Gasoline, 18
Hardison, W. L., 2, 146
Harley-Davidson Motor Co., 32
Harris Oils, 31, 38
Hasson, William, 144
Hastings Oil Filters, 103
Hats, 107–108, 129
HD Motor Oil, 30, 35
Headlamps, 113
Heart O' Pennsylvania Oil, 31

Heisman, John, 143
Heisman, Michael, 143
Higgins, Petillo, 146–147
Higher compression engines, 3
Higrade Cup Grease, 69
Holmden, Thomas, 137, 138
Homestead Well, 137
Hood Tires, 97, 103
Horse-drawn wagons, 142
Hubbard, O.P., 133
Hub cap, 113
Hudson Oil Company, 18
Humboldt Refinery, 137, 139
Huntington Beach oil wells, 146
Hyvis Motor Oils, Inc., 28, 63

Illinois Farm Bureau, 118
Illinois Oil Co., 18
Independent Oil Company, 44. See
    also Color Plates
Indian Motorcycle Company, 32,
    44
Indian Refining Company, 19, 23,
    32. See also Color Plates
Industrial Oil Corporation, 51, 70
Inkwells, 127
Instruction book, 114
Invader Motor Oil, 36, 39

Jack Nourse Oil Company, 30, 31,
    45, 55, 60, 64, 76
John Pritzfaff Hardware Company,
    56
Johnson Oil Refining Company, 32

Kansas, 147
Kelly Tires. See Color Plates
The Kemper Thomas Company, 96
Kendall Refining Company, 36, 39,
    44, 63, 104, 107
Kerosene pump, 4
Keynoil, 63
Keystone Lubricating Company, 45
Kier, Samuel M., 132, 133, 138
Klemco Cleaner, 66
Koolmotor Gasolene, 16, 116
The Kunz Oil Company, 97

Laessig, C. H., 4
Lake Shore Railroad, 143–144
Lesh's Arkoline Products, 42
Libbey Glass, 127
License plate attachments, 115,
    118
Light bulb, 102
Lighters, 117
Lincoln Shock Absorbers, 81
Lion Head Motor Oil, 32
Liquified petroleum gases, 140
Little Giant, 23
L.O. Church Corporation, 74
Lodge Spark Plugs, 82
Lord Calvert Auto Oil, 55
Low compression engines, 3
Lubricant containers, 68–73
Lubrication hats, 107–108
Lubrite Oil, 52
Lucas, Anthony F., 146–147
Ludovici brothers, 139

McElhenny, David, 135
Mack Trucks, 117
MacKeown and Finley, 133
MacKeown, William, 138–139
McPherson, Robert, 2, 146
Magic Gasoline, 83
Magnolia Mobiloil, 119. *See also*
    Color Plates
Magnolia Petroleum Company, 90,
    119. *See also* Color Plates
Manhattan Oil Company. *See*
    Color Plates
Map holders, 110–112
Maps, 110–112
Marathon Oil Co., 19, 82. *See also*
    Color Plates
Marshall Oil Company, 60
Martin & Schwartz Inc., 10, 13
Marvel Hi-Rev Motor Tune Up,
    75
Marx Toys, 124, 125
Master Trucks, Inc., 127
Maxim Motor Company, 128
Maxoil, 33
Mayo-Skinner Windshield Wipers,
    103
Meade, Moone, 134
Mellon, Andrew, 2, 147
Merrill, Joshua, 140
Metal signs, painted, 77, 78–79
Metro, 23
Michelin Tires, 94, 117. *See also*
    Color Plates
Micro-Lube Lubrication, 104
Midgley, Thomas, 3
Mirro Like Auto Products, 104
Mirror, 128
Mobil, 12, 19, 23, 24, 33, 34, 35,
    37, 40, 67, 69, 75, 82, 90,
    105, 108, 109, 119, 124. *See
    also* Color Plates
Model A Ford, 2
Model T Ford, 2
Mohawk Refining Company, 33,
    105
Mona Motor Oil, 45. *See also*
    Color Plates
Monarch Manufacturing Company,
    45. *See also* Color Plates
Monitor Oil Works, 143
Monogram Greases and Oils, 84
Montgomery Ward, 76
Moore's C-75 Motor Oil, 34
Mopar Parts, 85
Morris, Louis, 6
Mother Penn Motor Oil, 34
Motorists, 3–6
Motormeter Company Inc., 100
Motor oil. *See* Oil cans; Oil indus-
    try
Motor Tunometer, 113
Mountain State Motor Oil, 53
Mowbray, George M., 139
Murphy Oil Company, 4

Naphthas, 140
National Automobile Club, 90
National Carbon Company, Inc.,
    73
National Oil Company, 42

National Refining Company, 29,
    43, 59, 69
National Transit Company, 145
Natural gas, 143
Nellie Johnson No. 1 Well, 2
Neograph Phinney-Walker, 88
NevrNox Diamond Gasolene, 19
New Jersey Oil Company, 143
Niehoff Automotive Products, 105
Noble, Orange, 136
Noco Motor Oil, 30
Nourse Oil Company, 30, 31, 45,
    55, 60, 64, 76

Ocean Liner Motor Oil, 49, 53
Octane fuel, 3
O'Day, Daniel, 145
Ohio, 1–2
Oil bottles, 72, 105, 106
Oil cans. *See also* Color Plates
    five-gallon, 58–61
    five-gallon easy-pour, 62–64
    five-quart, 37–41
    half-gallon, 41–43
    one-gallon, 43–48
    one-quart, 28–37
    two-gallon, 48–58
Oil companies, 1–2. *See also* spe-
    cific names
Oil Creek Association, 136
Oil Creek Railroad, 142
Oil Creek Valley oil wells, 1,
    131–135, 138–139
Oil industry. *See also* Pennsylvania;
    specific oil company names
    automobile and, 2–3
    birth of, 131–132
    Bissell and, 133, 134, 143
    in California, 2, 146
    chain store tax and, 5
    coal boats and, 141
    collecting memorabilia from,
    6–7
    Drake and, 1, 131, 132, 134,
    138, 139
    early uses of oil and, 131
    European market and, 139
    Ferris and, 132–133, 138–139
    gas shortages of 1970s and, 5
    Great Depression and, 6
    Kier and, 132, 133, 138
    MacKeown and, 138–139
    motorists and, 3–6
    in Ohio, 1–2
    Oil Creek Association and, 136
    in Oklahoma, 2, 147
    petroleum geology and, 147
    Petroleum Producers Association
    and, 144
    Petroleum Refiners Association
    and, 144–145
    pipelines and, 142, 145, 146
    pond freshet and, 140–141
    railroads and, 142, 143–144,
    146
    refineries and, 137, 139–140,
    143, 144, 145
    refining technology and, 140
    Rockefeller and, 2, 143–146
    Sherman Antitrust Act and, 146

South Improvement Company
    and, 144
    teamsters and, 142
    in Texas, 2, 146–147
    transporting oil and, 140–144
    World War II and, 5
Oil ring, 106
Oilzum, 32, 67, 94, 95, 98
Oklahoma, 2, 147
OK Quality Used Cars and Trucks,
    95
One-gallon oil cans, 43–48
100% Pure Pennsylvania Oil, 24
One-quart oil cans, 28–37
Opaline Motor Oil, 45, 91. *See also*
    Sinclair Refining Company;
    Color Plates
Packard Motor Cars, 114
Palacine Oil Company, 42
Paper signs, 87–88
Paperweight, 128
Paraffin wax, 140, 143
Para-Field Motor Oil, 34
Parker, James, 139
Parlube Oil Company, 58
Pen and pencil set, 128
Penguin Motor Oil, 35, 52
Penn Airliner Motor Oil, 53
Pennant Motor Oil, 42
Penn-Bee Motor Oil, 29
Penn Champ Motor Oil, 36
Penn City–National Oil Company,
    49, 60
Penn Drake, 35, 36
Penn Empire Motor Oil, 64
Penn Hills Brand Industrial Oil
    Corporation, 57
Penn Refining Works, 6
Pennsyline Motor and Tractor Oils,
    54
Pennsylvania
    Allegheny River Valley oil wells
    and, 135–137
    Bradford oil wells and, 145–146
    oil companies with roots in, 1–2
    Oil Creek Valley oil wells and, 1,
    131–135, 138–139
    Petroleum Center oil wells and,
    143
    Pithole Creek oil wells and,
    137–138
    refineries in, 139–140
    transportation of oil in, 140–144
    Wildcat Hollow oil wells and,
    143
Pennsylvania Motor Oil, 57
Pennsylvania Oil Company, 58
Pennsylvania Penn Pool Oil, 51
Pennsylvania Petroleum Products
    Company, 50
Pennsylvania Rock Oil Company,
    1, 133, 134
Pennsylvania Sugar Company, 74
Penntroleum Motor Oil, 33
Pennzoil Company, 2, 6, 31, 34,
    35, 40, 46, 64, 79, 97, 123
Pep Boys, 70
Petroleum. *See* Oil industry
Petroleum Center oil wells, 143
Petroleum geology, 147

Petroleum jelly, 140
Petroleum Producers Agency, 145
Petroleum Producers Association, 144
Petroleum Refiners Association, 144–145
Philadelphia & Lake Erie Railroad, 142
Phillips Petroleum Company, 20, 29, 30, 35, 70, 111, 122, 128
Phillips, William, 135
P-H Lubricant Grease, 70
Pico Canyon oil wells, 2, 146
Piedmont Tire Service, Inc., 127
Pierce Petroleum Corporation, 42
Pins, 116
Pioneer Oil, 46
Pipelines, 142, 145, 146
Pithole Creek oil wells, 137–138
Pocketknife, 127
Polarine, 14, 61
Pond freshet, 140–141
Porcelain signs, 77, 89–92
Port Arthur exporting facility, 147
Power-lube Motor Oil, 91
Prather, George G., 137
Premiums. See Souvenirs
Premo Auto Oil sign, 82
Prentice, Frederick, 143
Prestone Anti-Freeze, 73, 99
Prices, 6
Primus Motor Oil, 54
Print, 127
Product displays, 99–107. See also Color Plates
Pump plates, 9, 22–26
Pump signs, 22–26, 79
Pure Oil Company, 2, 146
"Put a Tiger in Your Tank" banner, 86

Quaker Anti-Freeze Alcohol, 74
Quaker City Motor Oil, 31
Quaker State, 83

Radio, 126
Radio Oil Refineries Limited, 72
Railroads, 142, 143–144, 146
Ray Cotton Company, 127
Reading Railroad, 146
Red Bell Motor Oil, 54
Red Hat Gasoline. See Color Plates
"Red Lion" pinback, 116
Red Top Motor Oil, 42
Refineries, 137, 139–140, 143, 144, 145
Refining technology, 140
Resources for collectors, 148
Richfield Oil Corporation, 42, 46
Richlube Motor Oil, 42, 46
Road Boss Motor Oil, 56
Robert Bosch Pyro Action Spark Plugs, 80
Roberts torpedo, 143
Rockefeller, John D., 2, 143–146
Rocket Motor Oil, 55
Rock Island AntiKnock Gasoline, 20
Rose Bud Power Penn Gasoline, 20

Rotary drilling platform, 147
Rouse, Henry, 134
RPM Motor Oil Lubricants, 108
R. Toussaint & Co. See Color Plates
The Russian Oil Company, 47
Russolene Brand Motor Oil, 47
Ryan's Jet Hi-Test Gasoline. See Color Plates

Sales and service-related items. See also Color Plates
arm patches, 108–109
clocks, 94–95
hats, 107–108, 129
map holders, 110–112
maps, 110–112
miscellaneous, 113–114
product displays, 99–107
salesman's samples, 99–107
thermometers, 96–99
Salesman's samples, 99–107. See also Color Plates
Salt and pepper shakers, 121–122
Schaefer-Ross Company, Inc., 88
Schieffelins Brothers and Company, 139
Schrader Tire Gauge, 105
Scioto Sign Company, 80
Sea Chief, 24
Sears Roebuck and Company, 43
Security Oil Company, 14
Seneca Oil Company, 1, 133–134, 138, 139, 140
Service-related items. See Sales and service-related items
76 Union, 91
Shell Oil Company, 36, 52, 85, 106, 109, 124, 146. See also Color Plates
Sherman Antitrust Act (1890), 146
The Sico Company, 54
Signs. See also Color Plates
banners, 86–87
cardboard, 88
flanged, 83–85
function of, 77
light-up, 105
metal, painted, 77, 78–79
paper, 87–88
porcelain, 77, 89–92
pump, 22–26, 79
tin, painted, 77, 80–83, 100
Silliman, Benjamin, Jr., 133
Simonize Car Wax, 67
Sinclair, Harry, 147
Sinclair Opaline Motor Oil, 91. See also Color Plates
Sinclair Refining Company, 12, 20, 29, 35, 45, 91, 125. See also Color Plates
Skelly Oil Company, 21, 43, 47
Sky Chief, 24
The Slimp Oil Company, 46
Sliptivity Oil, 47
Smith, William A., 1
Socony-Vacuum Oil Company, Inc., 25, 33, 34, 40, 55, 72, 73, 87, 121
Solite Gasoline, 85

Southern Marketer, Inc., 21
South Improvement Company, 144
Souvenirs. See also Color Plates
ashtrays, 117
banks, 122–123
calendars, 119–121
collectibility of, 115
license plate attachments, 115, 118
lighters, 117
miscellaneous, 126–129
pins, 116
salt and pepper shakers, 121–122
toys, 124–125
Sovereign SS Gasoline, 21
Spindletop Well, 147
Standard Oil Company, 2, 3, 28, 61, 67, 71, 145
Stanocola Liquid Gloss, 67
Star Oil Company, 90
Steelcote Rubber Enamel, 106
Steel Super-X Oil Ring, 106
Stephens, George, 143
Sterling Oils, 25, 91
Stewart, Lyman, 2, 146
Strata Motor Oil, 50
Struthers, Thomas, 142
Studebaker Batteries, 95
Sturdy Motor Oil, 55
Suction pumps, 143
Sue Bland No. 1 Well, 2
Sunoco Oil Company, 13, 25, 26, 71, 106, 109, 123, 129
Sun Oil Company, 69, 71
Sunray Gasoline, 13
Superol Motor Oil, 33
Supply Company, 42
Supreme Cup Grease, 71

Tagliabue, Giuseppe, 140
Tagolene Motor Oil, 47
Tagolene Skelly Oil Co., 43
Tankar Special Motor Oil, 57
Tarr, James, 135–136
Teamsters, 142
Texaco, 2, 22, 24, 26, 71, 79, 92, 109, 112, 119, 125, 128, 129, 147
Texas, 2, 146–147
Texas Company, 2, 71, 119, 147. See also Texaco
Thermoil Lubricants Corporation, 29
Thermometers, 96–99
Thompson Products Aerotype Break-In Motor Oil, 34
Thompson Products, Inc., 34
Tidewater Oil Company, 1–2, 113, 146
Tidewater Pipe Company, 145–146
Tiger tails, 128
Tin banks, 123
Tin signs, painted, 77, 80–83
Tioga Gasoline, 13
Tiolene Oil, 72
Tiona Petroleum Company, 50
Tire gauge, 105

Tire rack, 105
Tokheim Dome Oil Pump, 4
Tokheim, John A., 4
Townsend, James M., 133
Tootsietoy, 124
Torpedo Gasoline, 18
Toys, 124–125
Track-siders, 4–5
Traffic Motor Oil, 56
Transcontinental Oil Company. *See* Color Plates
Traymore Lubricants, 48, 49, 53
Trop Artic Auto Oil, 29. *See also* Color Plates
Tru-Penn Motor Oil, 41
Tulane Motor Oil, 56
Tydol, 22, 26, 87, 118

Uncas Motor Oil, 57
Union Oil Company, 2, 91, 146
United States Petroleum Company, 137
United States Pipeline Company, 146

Vacuum Oil Company, 69
Vacuum still, 140
Valentine & Company, 98
Valentine's Automobile Varnishes, 98
Valley Oil Company Inc., 57
Valvoline Oil Company, 37, 44
Vanderbilt Premium Tires, 95
Vandergrift, Jacob Jay, 141, 144
Van Syckel, Samuel, 142
Veedol Motor Oils, 72, 85, 86, 87
Venango County Commissioners, 138
Vichrome Inc., 116

Wadhams Oil Company, 61
Waite Phillips Company, 69
Waltz, Louis, 6
Ward's Vitalized Engine Tone, 76
Warren-Teed Motor Oil, 57
Waxed cardboard banks, 123
Wearwell Aviation Gun Grease, 72
Weed Tire Chains. *See* Color Plates

Whippet Motor Oil, 58
White Eagle Oil and Refining Company, 63
The White & Bagley Company, 32, 67, 98
Whiz, 76, 107
Wildcat Hollow oil wells, 143
Wildcatters, 143
Wil-flo Motor Oil, 36
Willys Jeep, 92
Wolf's Head Oil, 48, 79, 129
Wolverine Lubricants Company, 48, 79, 129
Woodford, N.S., 135
Wright Oil Company, 53
Wyeth Hardware & Manufacturing Company. *See* Color Plates

X-Power, 107

Zephyr Motor Oil, 123
Zeppelin Motor Oil, 50
Zerolene, 92
Zeroniz Antifreeze, 74